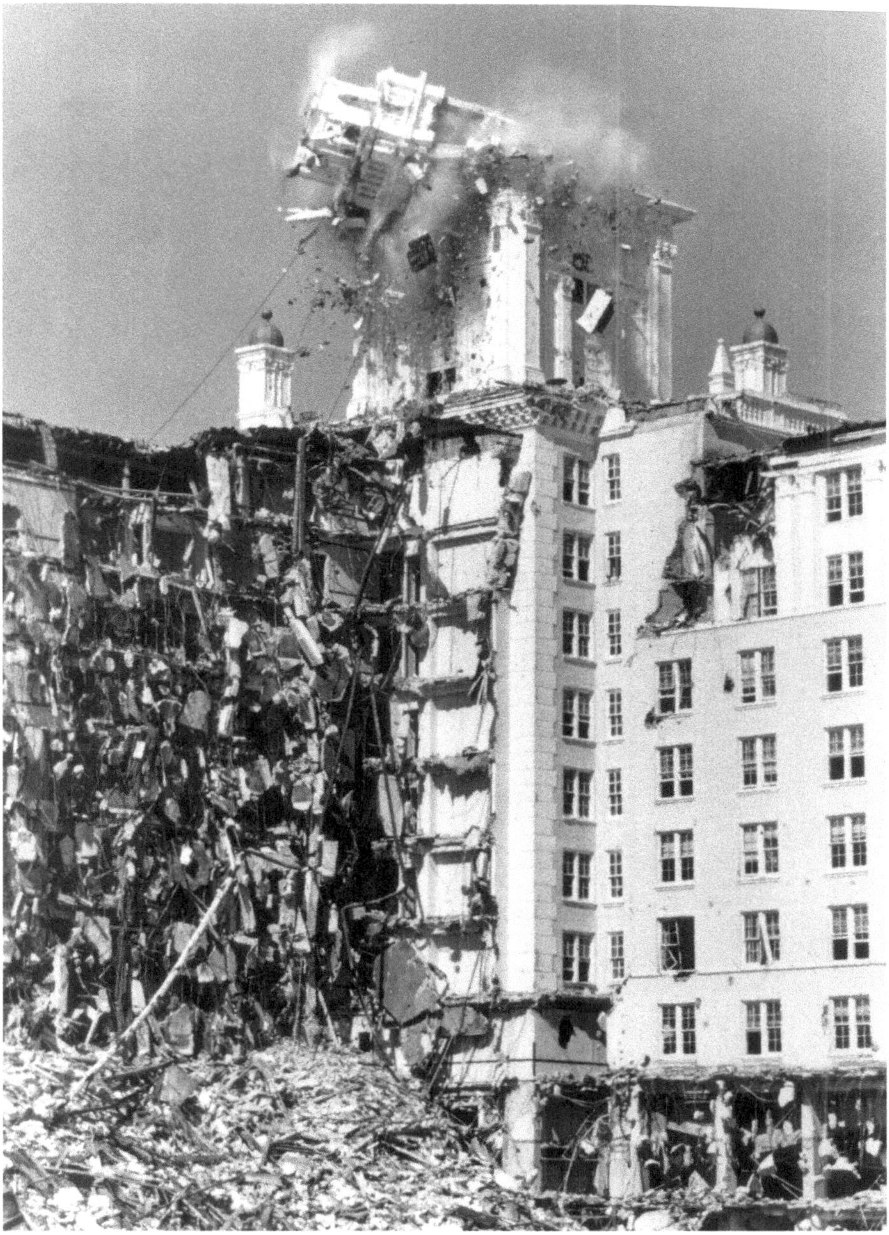

Roney Plaza Hotel demolition, 1968. *Courtesy Arva Moore Parks,* Miami News *collection.*

LOST
MIAMI BEACH

CAROLYN KLEPSER

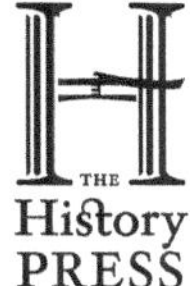

THE History PRESS

Published by The History Press
Charleston, SC 29403
www.historypress.net

Front cover: Postcard of the Roney Plaza Hotel. *Courtesy of Larry Wiggins.*
Back cover: Color postcard of the Roney Plaza Cabanas and Roman Pools Windmill.
Author's collection.

First published 2014

Manufactured in the United States

ISBN 978.1.62619.428.1

Library of Congress CIP data applied for.

Contents

ACKNOWLEDGEMENTS

Many people helped in this project, and my thanks go to all of you. To name a few in particular: My friend Larry Wiggins not only contributed images from his legendary postcard collection but also tracked down many answers to research questions and, with unfailing patience, helped me with the cybernetics. Equal thanks go to my friend and mentor Arva Moore Parks, who also gave generously from her photograph collection and provided scanning and computer help and always inspiring encouragement.

At the City of Miami Beach, which has a trove of treasures in its archive, special thanks go to Liliam Hatfield in the City Clerk's Office for her time and talent in mining these treasures and to Keith Valles for help with scanning. In the Planning Department, my thanks to Debbie Tackett, Michael Belush, James Murphy, Tui Munday and Laura Camayd for their help in accessing building records even when swamped with other duties.

At HistoryMiami, the regional museum formerly known as the Historical Association of Southern Florida, my gratitude goes to Rebecca Smith and Dawn Hugh in the research department for several images from their wonderful archive and to Ashley Trujillo for scanning them. At the Miami-Dade Public Library, for this and many other projects, John and Jennifer Shipley, Grisel Choter and others were unfailingly helpful with research and with images from another outstanding archive. Miami-Dade County should be ashamed of its relentless budget cuts to its library system.

Acknowledgements

Personal thanks go to Mr. Stanley Whitman for his kindness in sharing his firsthand memories, which brought the past to life for me, and to historian Dr. Paul George for his enthusiastic support and good advice: "Just start writing!"

Introduction

This book is perfect for armchair travelers, but it won't do much for tourism in Miami Beach. Most of the places it talks about are gone, so it's no use coming here to see them.

Why should we care about what is lost? Well, if there is any value in studying history at all, in order to have a complete picture of it, we need to fill in the blanks. For instance, photos of some long-forgotten buildings seem to indicate that the Moderne, or Art Deco, architectural style arrived here earlier than most people thought. In addition, looking at the reasons past treasures were destroyed—some understandable, some not—can influence our present decisions in city planning and inspire our efforts to preserve what matters most to us. Then, too, visiting the past is just plain interesting. Two things that struck me about the old days in writing this book are: *nobody was from here* and *they moved buildings a lot.*

There is, of course, a heavy emphasis on architecture here; we are mostly looking at old buildings. This seems especially appropriate in Miami Beach, a town that is synonymous with Art Deco, where both residents and tourists appreciate the built environment. But I hope that this book brings to light some of what was here long before the Depression-era building boom. Nostalgia is not the purpose of this writing. The main focus is on buildings that are not only gone but also lost to memory. Yes, I, too, remember Pumpernik's and Wolfie's and the mural in front of the Fontainebleau, but I would rather tell you about the Community Theatre, the Aquarium, the Miami Beach Garden and how the city limits changed. That said, I have also included some buildings that have only recently been torn down in order to make the point that historic preservation is still an ongoing debate.

This book will probably mean more to people familiar with Miami Beach, but even if you are not, there are some good stories here, and you can also look at broader topics such as how cities evolve and what was going on in this corner of the nation in the 1920s.

Space does not allow for as many photographs here as you would probably like or mention of everything that has been lost over the years. I apologize for all that had to be left out. With few exceptions, I have limited the topics here to things within Miami Beach. Yes, I, too, remember Motel Row in Sunny Isles, but that will have to be another book.

Fortunately, Miami Beach is young enough that cameras have been around for its entire history. Photographs are the closest things we have to a time machine. Still, they are only a visual record. Many other aspects of life have changed as much as the built environment: this was a world of screened sleeping porches, wool bathing suits and trolley bells. Cars—and their horns—sounded different and were still something of a luxury. Plane travel (and they weren't jets) was rare and miraculous. The most expensive hotel in town cost twenty-five dollars a night. There was no air conditioning as we know it, or sun block or electronics other than radio.

We live in our own time and can't save everything. Take all the pictures you can.

Chapter 1

Biscayne House of Refuge

Florida was the nation's last frontier, and it had much in common with the American West.

Both waged wars on their native populations. In Florida, the First Seminole War (1817–18) occurred under Spanish rule due to problems with border security. In 1821, Spain agreed to sell its Florida territory to the United States; then the Second Seminole War (1835–42) arose from Seminole resistance to forced relocation to the Arkansas and Oklahoma territories. Florida achieved statehood in 1845, the same year as Texas and five years before California.

In 1862, the U.S. government passed the Homestead Act for the purpose of settling federal lands in both Florida and the western territories. The act granted 160 acres of public land free to any adult citizen who improved it and lived on it for five years. Alternatively, one could purchase it for $1.25 per acre after only two years, but even this was a forbidding prospect in the steamy tropical wilderness of southern Florida

In 1860, the West had the Pony Express; in the 1880s, southern Florida had the Barefoot Mailman, who made a weekly round trip from Palm Beach to the Miami River (there was no Miami until 1896), a total of eighty miles on foot and fifty-six by rowboat or sail.

Both Florida and the West were opened up by the railroads. America's first transcontinental rail line traversed the West in 1869. In 1886, Standard Oil partner Henry Flagler began consolidating and constructing rail service down Florida's Atlantic coast, starting at Saint Augustine. What was eventually known as the Florida East Coast Railway reached Palm Beach in 1894 and the Miami River in 1896. By 1913, another 150 miles of track had been built through the Florida Keys to Key West, a thriving city for fifty years despite being accessible only by boat.

One problem in Florida that one didn't find so much out West was shipwrecks. The problem was not that ships would crash on rocks but rather that they would grind to a halt on the submerged reefs and constantly shifting sandbars and capsize, especially during storms. (We are talking about sailing ships here.) The crew and passengers could make it to shore, but on that desolate coast, they would soon perish of thirst and exposure. One such incident in October 1873 made national news when the crew from a wreck just north of present-day Miami Beach survived only because a beachcomber came across them.[1] Consequently, President Ulysses S. Grant ordered the United States Life-Saving Service (which became the Coast Guard in 1915) to construct a series of houses of refuge along the Florida coast. The first five were built in the winter of 1875–76; from north to south, they were called Bethel Creek (thirteen miles north of Fort Pierce), Gilbert's Bar (near Stuart), Orange Grove (Delray Beach), Fort Lauderdale and Biscayne (near present-day Seventy-second Street in Miami Beach).

By 1885, six more houses of refuge had been built in Florida, as well as two lifesaving stations (at Pensacola and Jupiter), whose mission was to go to the rescue of ships in distress. The houses of refuge were meant only to provide food, fresh water, clothing and lodging to stranded mariners and return them to civilization. The houses were two-story frame structures and were spaced approximately twenty-six miles from one another or from a lighthouse so a castaway would not have to travel more than thirteen miles one way or the other. Signs were posted along the beach to point the way to the nearest aid. Each house of refuge held enough provisions for twenty-five people for ten days. For safekeeping of the supplies, and to watch for wrecks and keep the signs in good repair, a keeper and sometimes his family lived in each refuge.[2]

All eleven of the Florida houses of refuge were built to the same plans, drawn by Francis Ward Chandler, architect for the Life-Saving Service, who was from Boston and a graduate of the Massachusetts Institute of Technology. In addition to the Florida structures, he designed lifesaving stations on the Pacific and Great Lakes coasts. The house of refuge buildings were of pine with cedar shingle roofs and were fifteen feet wide by thirty-seven feet long, plus an eight-foot-wide veranda that wrapped around three

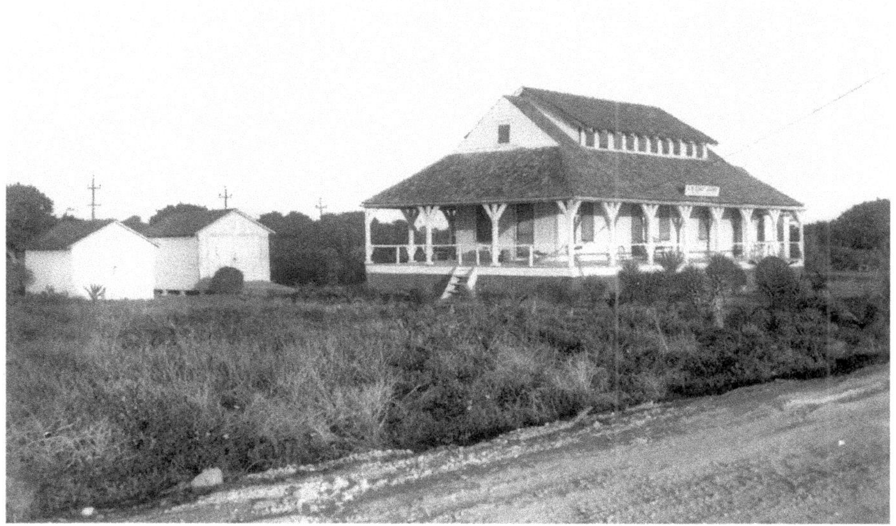

The Biscayne House of Refuge as a U.S. Coast Guard Station in 1925, with the "beach road" in the foreground. *Courtesy Miami-Dade Public Library, Gleason Romer archive 7B.*

sides.[3] Each site also had an observation tower, a privy, sheds and a boathouse for the keeper's use.

Hannibal D. Pierce, who had left Chicago during its Great Fire, was the first keeper of the Orange Grove House of Refuge at Delray Beach. His son Charles describes the house in his memoir, *Pioneer Life in Southeast Florida*:

> *The houses of refuge were built to withstand storms and hurricanes. The foundation was framework of 8 by 8 timber placed some three or four feet in the ground: onto this framework were mortised 8 by 8 posts that in turn were mortised into the sills and held there by large wooden pins. The roof extended over the porches on each side of the building…The porch at the north end was enclosed for a kitchen and supplied with a fireplace and brick chimney. This chimney proved a source of much trouble later on: it smoked badly when there was a strong wind from the northwest or north as the chimney was too short for a proper draft.*
>
> *All of these houses were built exactly alike, and all of the keepers used the four rooms on the ground floor in the same order as we did. The south room was a bedroom and the next was always used as a living room; the next was a dining room and then the kitchen. North of the kitchen was the cistern, built in the ground and made of brick. Eave troughs led from*

> *the house to this cistern, which was the only water supply furnished by the government. The shingles were new unseasoned cypress and when we arrived the cistern was full of water from this new roof. It was brown in color, bitter, and with a strong cypress flavor, more like medicine than drinking water.*
>
> *The house...had a second story dormitory for shipwrecked sailors.*[4]

A few years later, in 1883, Hannibal Pierce was appointed keeper of the Biscayne house. Charles worked as his assistant and describes the keeper's duties:

> *There was not much to do except keep a lookout for anything that might appear in sight on the ocean or on the beach. We had to keep the log and enter in it the number of brigs, barks, ships, and steamers that passed each day. We also entered the state of the weather and sea and the direction of the wind. We made barometer and thermometer readings three times a day. The service asked that these records be kept, yet it did not furnish any of the instruments. We happened to have a good barometer that belonged to my uncle and a thermometer of our own, so we kept proper records.*[5]

A highlight of Pierce's term at Biscayne was when the coconut planters came through. In 1882, New Jersey entrepreneurs Elnathan Field, Ezra Osborn and Henry Lum had purchased about sixty miles of oceanfront land extending from Key Biscayne to Jupiter, Florida, and planned to start a coconut plantation. Coconuts were valued for coir, the husk fiber used to make rope, and copra, which produces oil. Very few coconut palms were growing naturally in this area at that time. Over three years, this group hired a schooner to bring more than 330,000 coconuts from Trinidad, Nicaragua and Cuba and had a team of off-season Atlantic City lifeguards plant them along this trackless coast. Because there was no customs officer in the area, the Key West customhouse appointed Hannibal Pierce to supervise the offloading of the coconuts in 1883. Charles helped with the planting and recounts it in his memoir. The coconut plantation failed, but this was an important episode in Miami Beach history because one of the New Jersey investors in the project was city founder John S. Collins.

John Thomas (Jolly Jack) Peacock, an Englishman who settled in Coconut Grove, succeeded Hannibal Pierce as keeper of the Biscayne house from February 1885 to July 1890. His son Richard Peacock was born there on November 4, 1886, the first recorded birth in what would become Miami

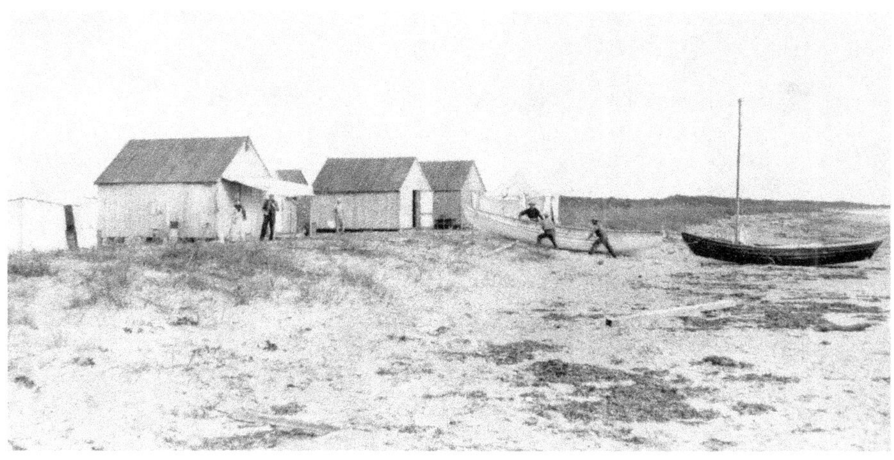

The coconut planters in the 1880s would dismantle these shacks and reassemble them as they progressed along the coastline. *Courtesy Arva Moore Parks, Ralph Munroe collection.*

Beach. William H. Fulford, a former ship's captain, was the next keeper at Biscayne, from July 1890 to April 1902. The *Miami Metropolis* reported that he killed a nine-foot crocodile behind the house of refuge in 1896, with two rounds from a shotgun:

> *For some time the beast had been permitted the freedom of the grounds as a sort of pet, but on the day he was killed he was in a savage mood and was lashing the water furiously a short distance away from where Capt. and Mrs. Fulford were making a landing.*[6]

During his service, Fulford acquired one of those 160-acre tracts under the Homestead Act in the area of present-day 163rd Street; it later became the town of Fulford. After he left the house of refuge, Captain Fulford was his town's first postmaster. The town of Fulford was renamed North Miami Beach in 1931.

The last keeper of the Biscayne house was Laurence F. (Frank) Tuten, who took over in 1917. By that time, Miami Beach was already a city a few miles to the south, and the house of refuge had outlived its original purpose. The Coast Guard officially discontinued it after World War I, but Tuten stayed on there with his family until the September 1926 hurricane, keeping a lookout for rumrunners during Prohibition. He needed only to turn his spyglass landward; by the early 1920s, a two-story log house known as the Jungle Inn stood just a few hundred yards away, at what is now the southeast

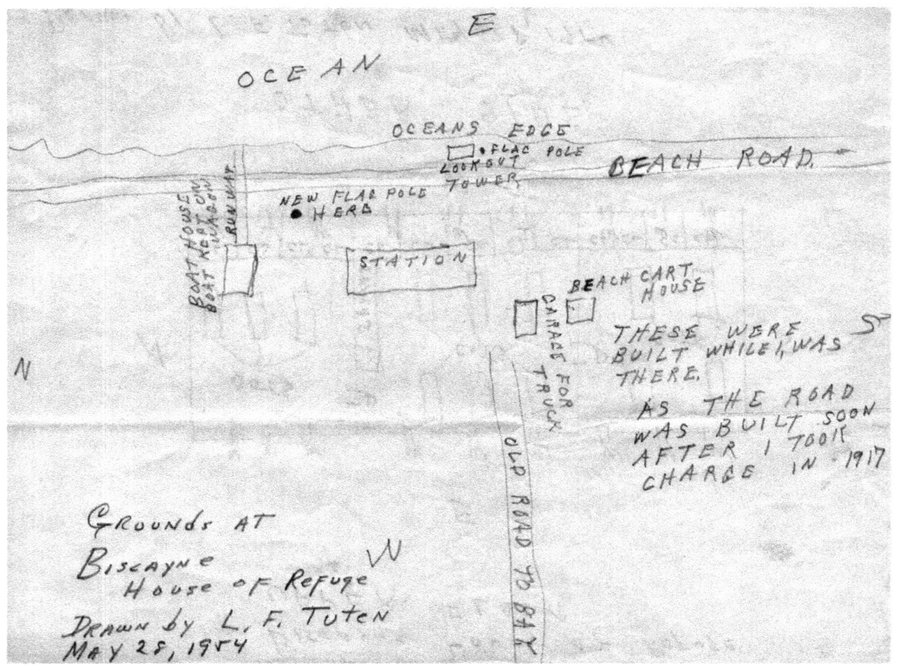

The sketch of the Biscayne House of Refuge site that its last keeper, Frank Tuten, drew from memory. *Courtesy HistoryMiami.*

corner of Abbott Avenue and Sixty-ninth Street. Outside the city limits and surrounded by empty land, it was a notorious speakeasy and had a gambling parlor upstairs. An exposé in the *Miami Metropolis* led to a raid in 1923.[7]

Tuten's wife, Helen, died in 1925. During the hurricane the following year, Tuten and his young son narrowly escaped as the house of refuge blew off its foundations.[8]

In 1954, when he was interviewed for an article in the *Miami Herald*, Frank Tuten made a pencil sketch of the Biscayne House of Refuge site that is now in the HistoryMiami archive. What is interesting about this sketch is that it shows a "beach road," with Tuten's notation that "the road was built soon after I took charge in 1917." There will be more about this road in Chapter 5. It was built by the Tatum brothers.

Bethel B., Johnson R. and Smiley M. Tatum were Georgia boys. Bethel moved to Florida in 1881 at age seventeen and worked in the newspaper business. Johnson Tatum, two years younger, went to business college and moved to Miami in 1911, working in banking and insurance. The third brother, Smiley, was a chemist for many years in Bartow, Florida, until acid fumes injured his eyes. He moved to Miami in 1902.[9]

In Miami, the brothers formed a number of realty and investment firms, platted several subdivisions there and, in Florida City, developed vast tracts of the Everglades. The Tatums Ocean Park Company owned most of the oceanfront land north of the Biscayne House of Refuge, extending up to Fulford (163rd Street), but it was difficult to access. On September 11, 1917, the Tatums and other property owners gained from the Dade County Commission the right of way to build a coastal road from the Miami Beach city limits, which were then near present-day 46th Street, up to the beach adjacent to Fulford, a stretch of about seven miles, in order to access their land. After the road went through, the Tatums began, in 1919, to plat their six Altos del Mar subdivisions, followed by Ocean Beach Heights in what is now Bal Harbour and Tatums Ocean Beach Park in what is now Sunny Isles.

In 1922, at the Tatums' request, a land survey was conducted in the vicinity of the house of refuge because they felt they were being taxed for more land than they owned. The tax outcome is unknown, but the survey revealed that the Biscayne House of Refuge had been constructed about two hundred feet south of its tract of U.S. government land. The Treasury Department took bids for moving it; accepted one on February 12, 1923;[10] and shortly thereafter, the house and its outbuildings were hauled no farther than necessary to the south end of the government property. It is really not surprising that the house had been built out of place since there were no landmarks at that time and surveying was rather hit or miss.

(The Fort Lauderdale House of Refuge had also been built off its intended site because the lumber for its construction had been floated ashore, and the ocean currents carried it a mile and a half to the north. The house was built where the lumber landed, which was easier than carrying it back. In 1891, while undergoing repairs, that house, too, was moved to its proper location.)[11]

After fifty years, the Biscayne House of Refuge had become obsolete, and it was torn down after the 1926 hurricane damaged it beyond repair. The local Coast Guard station placed a new bronze plaque at its site at Seventy-second Street in 2004. The only house of refuge still standing is the one at Gilbert's Bar near Stuart, Florida, which is now a museum.

CHAPTER 2
OCEAN BEACH

Many people built Miami Beach. At the beginning, Elnathan Field, Ezra Osborn and Henry Lum bought the land for their coconut plantation in the 1880s. Henry Lum died in 1895, and his portion of land went to his son Charles.

In 1901, four years before the Government Cut shipping channel opened, Richard M. Smith built a two-story wooden pavilion on Lum's land, on the beach just north of where the cut would be. It had a high, pyramidal roof, but the sides were open and there were no amenities. It was mostly a shelter from sun and rain for the people from Miami who came by boat for a day at the beach. In 1908, Avery Smith from Connecticut (no relation to Richard) visited the site, as he later recounted:[12]

> *I stood on the shore of Biscayne Bay and looked across to where Miami Beach now is. All one could see was an impenetrable curtain or mass of mangrove trees reaching as far north and south as vision could discern… Our only guide through the tangled mass was an occasional view of the roof of an old building that had been built there as a clubhouse by one Dick Smith, an old-time city clerk of Miami. The building was mostly roof, very high and shaped like the famous pyramids of Egypt, and it served us well as a guide through the jungle.*

At that time, Henry M. Black of New York owned the building and leased the land where it stood from Charles Lum of Red Bank, New Jersey. Avery

Smith saw an opportunity to develop a resort on this swampy peninsula across the bay from Miami, so he bought the building from Black and had Lum transfer the land lease to him. "I then became owner of the only building at the beach," Smith recalled, "and held lease on the strip of land 132 feet wide north [to] south, and extending from ocean to bay, the entire width of the island."

Smith returned to Connecticut, where he operated excursion steamers in the summers. "This was what I liked best of all," he said. There, in 1909, he persuaded a friend, James C. Warr of Wareham, Massachusetts, to join in his Florida venture, "to develop a day pleasure resort" and start a boat service to reach it:

> *We formed a partnership called the Biscayne Navigation Company and in the fall of 1909 came to Florida and started building boats and wharves at Miami and at the beach, as well as bath houses and boardwalks, this being really the beginning of Miami Beach, so far as its becoming a city was concerned.*

The original building, with its pointed roof, remained intact for many years, expanded and improved as Smith's Casino. (The term "casino" just means "small house" and had nothing to do with gambling.) At some point, Smith related, without explanation,

> *our ferry franchise was suddenly revoked* [and] *opposition resulted…As the unpleasantness occasioned by opposition became evident, my partner, Mr. Warr, wished to retire, and I bought out his interests, taking on the fight single-handed, a fight which lasted a number of years.*

The Ocean Beach Company

Charles Lum owned more land to the north of the tract that Smith was leasing. The Lummus brothers, James E. and John N., Miami bankers, became interested in it after John Collins approached them for a loan to build a bridge across the bay. This was about 1912, and Smith was already running ferry service to his bathhouse at the south end of the peninsula. The Lummuses saw the opportunity, especially once there was a bridge, to create a resort north of Smith's that they would call Ocean Beach.

In 1912, the Lummus brothers, together with Avery Smith and others, formed the Ocean Beach Realty Company and bought nearly six hundred acres of this land, most of it from Lum. Biscayne Street (sometimes called Biscayne Avenue) was laid out along the north side of Smith's strip of land, and the numbered streets started a block farther north. In July 1912, the Ocean Beach Realty Company began platting and selling the Ocean Beach Subdivision. It started at Biscayne Street and went north to Fifth Street; from east to west, it went only two blocks, from Ocean Drive to what would become Washington Avenue.

But the Ocean Beach project was out of cash. In early 1913, J.N. Lummus borrowed $150,000 from Carl G. Fisher, a multimillionaire from Indiana who would become the main developer of Miami Beach in the 1920s. There will be much more to come about Fisher.

In exchange for financial and logistical help in developing Ocean Beach, Lummus gave Fisher over one hundred acres at the north end of his land. Fisher set to work clearing and filling in the swampy Ocean Beach property. By November 1914, the Ocean Beach Subdivision and its four additions covered most of the land, such as it was, from Biscayne Street to Fifteenth Street, from the ocean to what would be Alton Road.

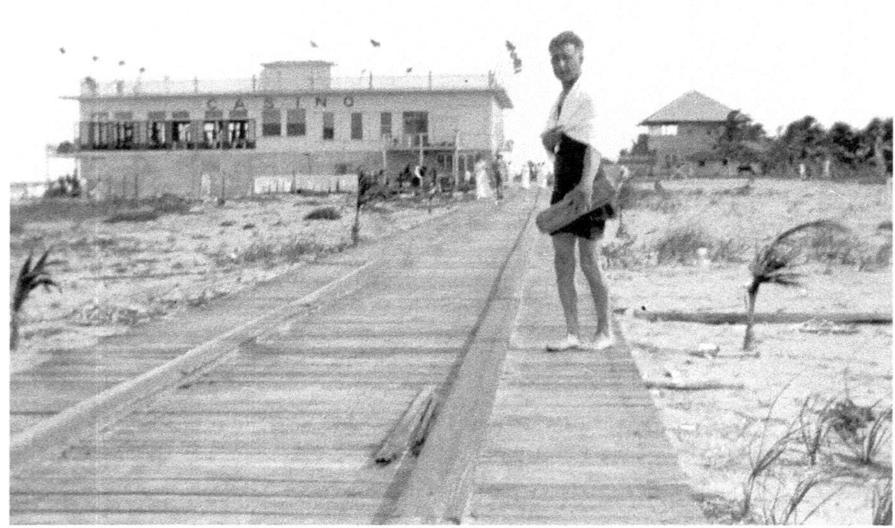

Smith's (right) and Hardie's Casinos, pre-1920, on the boardwalk at the south end of the beach. *Courtesy Arva Moore Parks.*

The avenues in Ocean Beach were originally named for fruits and trees—from east to west, Lemon, Banana, Orange, Pine, Palm, Mango and Pear. A city ordinance in 1927[13] changed them to Drexel, Pennsylvania, Euclid, Meridian, Jefferson, Michigan and Lenox.

In April 1913, Smith's Casino got some competition. Dade County sheriff Dan Hardie opened a rival bathhouse with a restaurant a block north of Smith's. Hardie's was at first a plain, two-story flat-roofed building. By 1918, both casinos had added swimming pools, filled with seawater circulated by pumps. By 1920, Hardie's Casino had expanded and got a new, distinctive façade on Ocean Drive, with two square towers with peaked tile roofs complementing the Smith Casino pyramid.

The office of the Ocean Beach Realty Company was a one-story wood-frame building at the northeast corner of Ocean Drive and Biscayne Street, between the two casinos. It was there that J.N. Lummus, John Collins and Carl Fisher incorporated Miami Beach as a town on March 26, 1915. It had thirty-three registered voters. J.N. Lummus was elected the first mayor. Soon, a two-story town hall was built at 609 Collins Avenue, and Scotsman William J. Brown opened the town's first hotel, which is still standing, on Ocean Drive at First Street. It was also at about this time that Avery Smith built his small "coral rock" house in Ocean Beach, on Collins Avenue at Ninth Street, which has miraculously managed to survive.

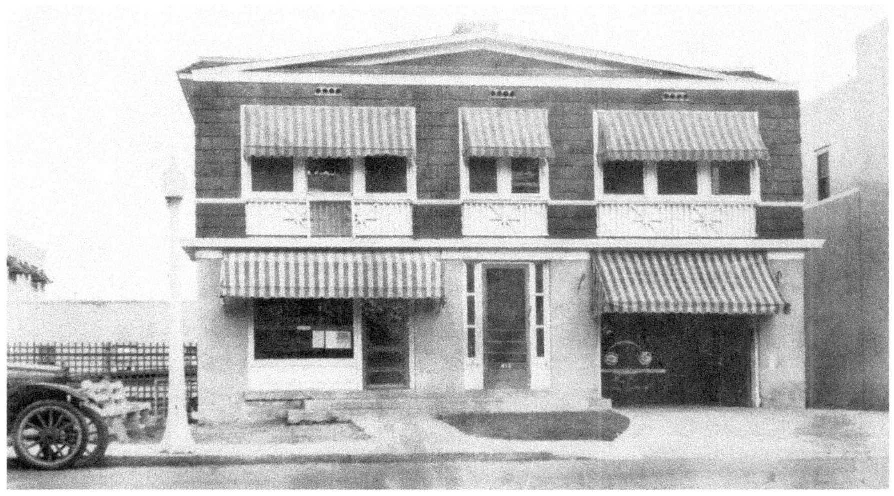

The first city hall for Miami Beach, at 609 Collins Avenue, seen here in 1924. The fire truck occupied the right side. *Courtesy City of Miami Beach Historical Archive.*

Then the Ocean Beach project seemed to stall. Collins had finished his bridge, but land sales were slow, and plans for a causeway from Miami to the Lummus part of town were delayed by World War I. In April 1916, the Lummus brothers, who had land but little money, joined forces with Carl Fisher, who had the opposite problem, and others to form the Miami Ocean View Company. Avery Smith, who was still leasing his land from Lum, seems to have been left out of Miami Ocean View. President of the company was oil millionaire James Snowden, who had just bought an oceanfront tract from John Collins where he would build his fabulous estate. "With the organization of the Miami Ocean View Company," writes Howard Kleinberg, "Fisher had for all practical purposes bought out most of Lummus' holdings."[14] By 1917, the town had grown enough to become the city of Miami Beach. With the end of the war and the prosperity of the 1920s came the Florida land boom. In Miami Beach, after Fisher's company filled in the land and mounted a publicity campaign, and the County Causeway provided additional roadway access and trolley service, development took off.

RECONFIGURING THE LAND

One thing Miami Beach lost long ago was its original topography. Today, about half of its acreage is manmade—either waterways carved out of the original landmass or new land created from dredged-up bay bottom.

Before there was a Miami Beach, this was a peninsula along the ocean, about twelve miles long and terminating to the south at Norris Cut. Biscayne Bay, about three miles wide, separated it from the mainland. Indian Creek split the peninsula from north to south, entering from the bay at present-day Sixty-seventh Street and continuing down to Twenty-fourth Street. At one time, it washed into the ocean there, but by the twentieth century, this outlet had silted up.

Across the bay, the City of Miami's quest for a direct shipping channel brought about the first incursion into the geography. In 1905, Government Cut severed the south end of the peninsula, creating what is now called Fisher Island.

Miami Beach pioneer John Collins wrought the second major change to the landscape in 1912 with the Collins Canal, connecting the south end of Indian Creek to the bay. The following year, the Collins Bridge was the first causeway across the bay, which at that time was open water except for Bull's Island. At the east end of the canal, the Collins company bulkheaded and dredged Lake Pancoast and removed an island in Indian Creek near Thirty-third Street.

The west side of the peninsula was mostly a tangled mangrove swamp. As early as 1913, the Lummus brothers had begun clearing their land at the south end and filling it with sand dredged from the bay. This process was taken to a greater extreme by Carl G. Fisher, who influenced the creation of Miami Beach more than any other developer. He filled in Bull's Island and, in 1914, renamed it Belle Isle to make it more marketable. In 1916, Fisher's company took over much of the Lummus land and continued the dredging and filling of the bay front. Six million cubic yards of fill were brought in. In 1920, a second causeway was completed across the bay at Fifth Street, built on fill dredged up from Government Cut.

A 1935 map[15] documents the original landmass of Miami Beach up to Sixty-second Street. It shows the original shoreline of the bay in South Beach at Washington Avenue up to Sixth Street; then angling northwestward to Michigan Avenue at Fifteenth Street; then north through the middle of the Bay Shore Golf Course; along the Biscayne Waterway; and then through the La Gorce Golf Course. Everything to the west of that line was filled in. In the north part of the city, the original landmass extended from the ocean only as far as Dickens Avenue.

In the process of deepening the bay to create a racecourse for speedboats and channels for Fisher's clients' yachts, islands were almost accidentally created from the dredgings. It didn't take long to realize that lucrative new real estate could be created by pumping the fill into retaining walls. First Flagler (Monument) and Star Islands and then Palm and Hibiscus Islands were formed in this way. In 1923, Fisher dug out Sunset Lake, turning what were four small peninsulas into the Sunset Islands. Farther north, Fisher carved out Surprise Lake and its three waterways, and in 1924, he dredged up Allison and La Gorce Islands and built the first bridge across Indian Creek. Several miles to the north, in April 1925, a cut was completed at Baker's Haulover that linked bay to ocean and forever changed the tidal flow.

Also in the early 1920s, the Collins Bridge was replaced by the more substantial Venetian Causeway, and five additional islands were constructed on it, west of Belle Isle: Rivo Alto, DiLido and San Marino were in Miami Beach; San Marco and Biscayne were within the Miami city limits.

At the north end of the city, Biscayne Point was created in the bay in 1925, and developer Henri Levy began dredging and filling in the south half of the former Meade Island to create Normandy Isle. In 1929, on Levy's initiative, a third causeway crossed the bay there. Another point, Biscayne Beach, reached into the bay at Eighty-fourth Street in 1947. Johns and Collins Islands and the bay front at Forty-first Street were filled in as the Mount Sinai Medical Center grew, and the Julia Tuttle Causeway, the city's fourth, was built in 1959.

South Beach Park and the Smith Company

South of Ocean Beach, casino owner Avery Smith appears to have continued operating independently on his leased land. Then, in September 1920, all of the Lum property south of Biscayne Street, including Smith's 132-foot-wide strip and more, was surveyed and, in December, was platted as the South Beach Park Subdivision. The platting was done anonymously, but a realty ad at the time[16] identifies the owners of South Beach Park as James R. Reid and Wade H. Harley. Reid (1863–1929) was from Bowling Green, Ohio, and came in 1911 to Miami, where he developed the Bay Shore Subdivision.[17] Harley (1888–1963), "pioneer Miami real estate man,"[18] came to Miami in 1904 from South Carolina. In South Beach Park, these two laid out Harley Street one block south of Biscayne Street and Reid Place running along the oceanfront. In 1928, the Kennel Club obliterated both these streets.

In 1921, Avery Smith founded the Smith Company, Incorporated, together with his friend James Warr, who came back, and Miami banker Charles L. Briggs. Briggs was from Haverhill, Massachusetts, where he had owned a tannery, and had interests in New York and Boston banks. By 1926, he owned a paper mill in New York State, and in Miami, he was a partner in Briggs and Warr, real estate.[19]

As Smith later recalled, "We then purchased the Charles S. Lum strip of land, upon which I had built many buildings, and had operated under the original lease with extensions of time."[20] The many buildings he refers to included improvements to his casino. It was more than a bathhouse for beachgoers; by this time, it had a 300,000-gallon swimming pool, and a two-story frame building stretching for half a block along Biscayne Street that architect George Dickens designed in 1921. It had a number of concessions and a dance floor.

In addition, in 1923 and 1924, the Smith Company had built a colony of thirty-six one-story frame houses on Smith's strip of land on the west side of Washington Avenue. They were known as Smith's Cottages, and each had a living room, dining room, kitchen, bedroom, bath and garage. They were low-cost rentals, "for the independent housing of those not caring for hotel life, or who, we may say, in some instances are unable to pay hotel prices."[21] Smith may have intended these as housing for his own employees, an amenity that was in short supply in other developments, particularly Fisher's. Smith's Cottages, as well as Smith's Casino, were torn down in 1951.

In 1924, Avery Smith sold his interests in the Smith Company to his partners, although the company still kept his name. Briggs became president, Warr was treasurer and Harold Holmes was secretary. Soon, they added a hotel and a movie theater to Smith's old tract of land.

The hotel was the Warr Inn, a name sometimes corrupted to the Hotel Warrinn, on the southeast corner of Collins Avenue and Biscayne Street. George L. Pfeiffer, a German architect who moved to Miami from Chicago in 1909, designed it in 1925. Three stories tall, it had eighty-eight rooms and ten storefronts and cost $100,000. The Warr Inn, later known as the Beach End Hotel, was demolished in 1964.

The gem of the neighborhood was the Biscayne Plaza Theatre, on the southwest corner of Collins Avenue and Biscayne Street. It was the city's second movie house, designed for the Smith Company in 1926 by architect George E.T. Wells. In 1913, Wells had studied at the École des Beaux-Arts in Paris. In 1924, he came to Miami, where, within two years, he designed the Exchange Building, the Robert Clay and Columbus Hotels and the Capitol Theatre.[22]

The *Miami Herald* raved: "The Biscayne Plaza Theater [*sic*], valued at $300,000 and seating 1,500 people, marks a new epoch in the amusement facilities in Miami Beach."[23] Belying its cavernous interior space, the entrance on Biscayne Street was a charming little one-story structure. Its architecture was described as "Spanish," but there was plenty of Beaux-Arts influence. The box office was set into a high, rounded arch, its shape echoed in the parapet above, which was trimmed with latticework and emblazoned with "an electrical display sign" spelling out the theater's name in light bulbs. Beneath the sign were cast-stone busts of "six gaiety girls, three to a side," and a dome on the roof, "which is studded with crystals, is flooded with light from hidden sources."

The building permit for the Biscayne Plaza was issued in February 1926, and it was still under construction when the hurricane hit in September. The Kimball organ that had just been installed was damaged in the storm and went back to the factory; while awaiting a replacement, a piano was substituted, together with a full symphony orchestra that performed regularly. The theater opened on Thanksgiving evening, November 25, 1926, with the Universal film *The Old Soak*. The feature the next week was *Kosher Kitty Kelly*. They were, of course, silent. The Biscayne Plaza was demolished in 1960.

The last of the Smith Company's big projects was the Miami Beach Kennel Club, or dog track. Owen P. Smith (no relation to the other two Smiths) had introduced greyhound racing to Florida in 1921. He had invented the mechanical rabbit that overcame humane concerns about using live rabbits in the sport and increased its acceptance. Once Florida legalized parimutuel gambling, Hialeah developers Glenn Curtiss and James Bright brought Smith to Miami[24] and built the Biscayne Kennel Club near Miami Shores.

New York sports promoter Tex Rickard worked with Owen Smith to bring the sport to Miami Beach. The track was built in 1928 south of Smith's Casino, in the South Beach Park Subdivision, and became a local landmark. The grandstand and clubhouse were designed by Robert Law Weed early in his career (Weed's biography is in Chapter 6). The two-story, tile-roofed clubhouse was described as "an architectural masterpiece, patterned after an old Spanish mission…a fitting background for the 'Sport of Queens.'"[25]

The original Miami Beach Kennel Club was replaced with a new building in 1960, which was, in its turn, also demolished.

Hotels in Ocean Beach

As Ocean Beach began to prosper with tourism, hotels proliferated to meet the demand. Most of those from this early period are now gone.

The William Penn Hotel went up in 1924 on a triangular lot where Washington and Pennsylvania Avenues converge. Though only four stories tall, it had a commanding presence. Architects were Harvey & Clarke. It was Mediterranean style, with frills at the parapet and small

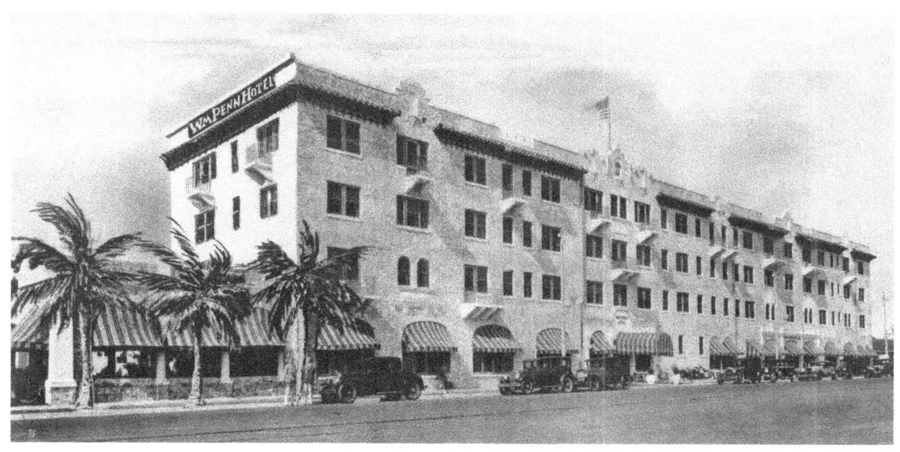

The Mediterranean-style William Penn Hotel was built in 1924 where Washington and Pennsylvania Avenues meet. *Courtesy City of Miami Beach Historical Archive.*

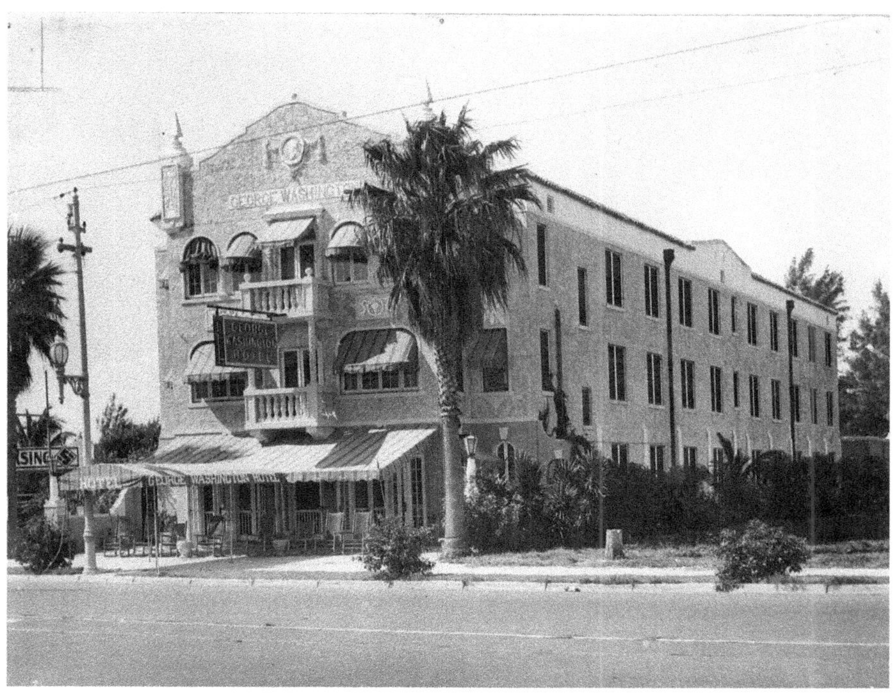

The George Washington Hotel, at 516 Washington Avenue, was designed by William F. Brown in 1924. *Courtesy City of Miami Beach Historical Archive.*

projecting masonry balconies and long sections of projecting barrel-tile roof that looked like a precursor to the eyebrows of the Art Deco style. It had 102 rooms and two elevators and cost $325,000. The William Penn was demolished in 1976.

Also built in 1924 on Washington Avenue at Fifth Street was the George Washington Hotel, designed by William F. Brown. With three stories and fifty-seven rooms, it cost $75,000. The front façade shows Beaux-Arts features in its fancy parapet, portrait medallion with swags, bas-relief panels, finials, round-arched windows and stone balustrades. It survived until the 1980s.

The designer, WILLIAM F. BROWN (1886–1952), was one of the pioneer architects in Miami Beach. A native of London, England, Brown had previously been a seaman and had traveled around the world. Brown came to Miami Beach around 1922 and was employed by Carl Fisher.[26] In addition to his many buildings in this part of town, Brown also designed, in 1926, Carl Fisher's Boulevard Hotel, discussed in Chapter 9. Among his surviving work is the Bastian Building at 835 Lincoln Road, built in 1925.

In 1925, Brown also designed the Biscayne-Collins Hotel, on the northeast corner of Collins Avenue and Biscayne Street, directly across from the Smith Company's Warr Inn. The Biscayne-Collins had three stories plus a small rooftop pavilion of open, rounded arches. Two wings framed a front courtyard, and the roof was flat. In Beaux-Arts fashion, the building was ornamented with quoins, stone balustrades, decorative shields and swags and spiraled finials at the corners. As the photo shows,

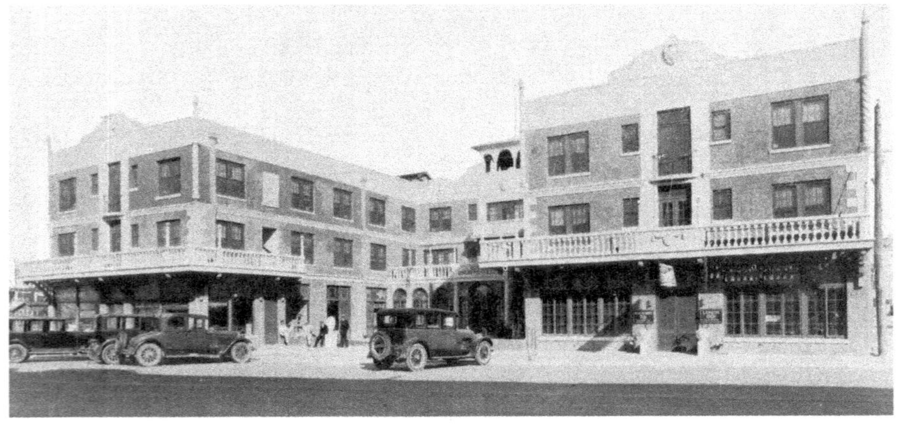

The Biscayne-Collins Hotel at 125 Biscayne Street, built in 1925. *Courtesy Arva Moore Parks.*

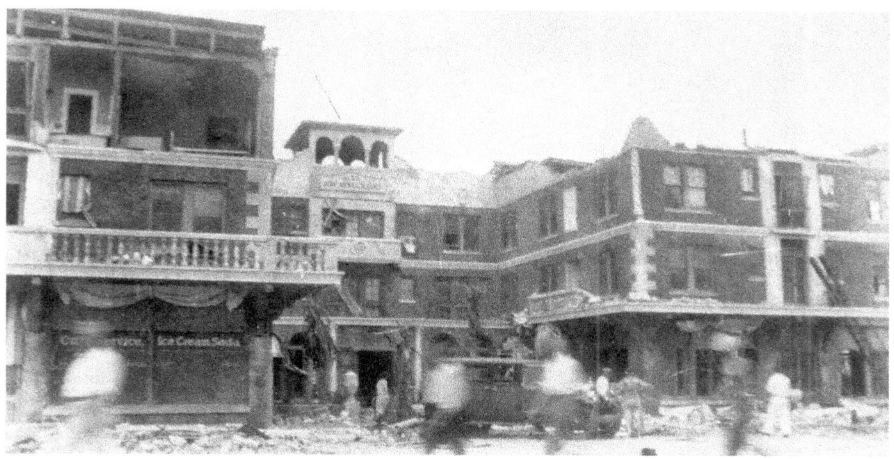

The Biscayne-Collins after the hurricane, September 1926. *Courtesy City of Miami Beach Historical Archive.*

many of these features were lost in the 1926 hurricane, but the hotel survived until 1984.

The area of Miami Beach south of Fifth Street had a large Jewish population because Lummus policies were more welcoming than those of the other developers. In July 1925, Vilma B. Granat, who was from Hungary, built the David Court Hotel at 56 Washington Avenue, at the corner of Commerce Street. The architect is not recorded, but this was an impressive three- and four-story Mediterranean building with two tile-roofed towers framing a central courtyard. It cost $90,000. Before it could be built, though, a frame-stucco bungalow that stood on the site had to be moved. It went to a lot that Mrs. Granat owned over a mile away on Sheridan Avenue. Carl Fisher's wife, Jane, later lived in the house, and it still stands, although the David Court was demolished in 1987.[27]

Cook's Casino and Carter's Pier

In the spring of 1926, construction started on Miami Beach's fourth bathing casino, Cook's, at the east end of Fifth Street, a few blocks north of Smith's and Hardie's. It measured over fifteen thousand square feet and cost $80,000.

The owner was John Cook Jr., who had operated the Eureka Baths that his father built in Brooklyn, New York, in the early 1900s. John Jr. moved

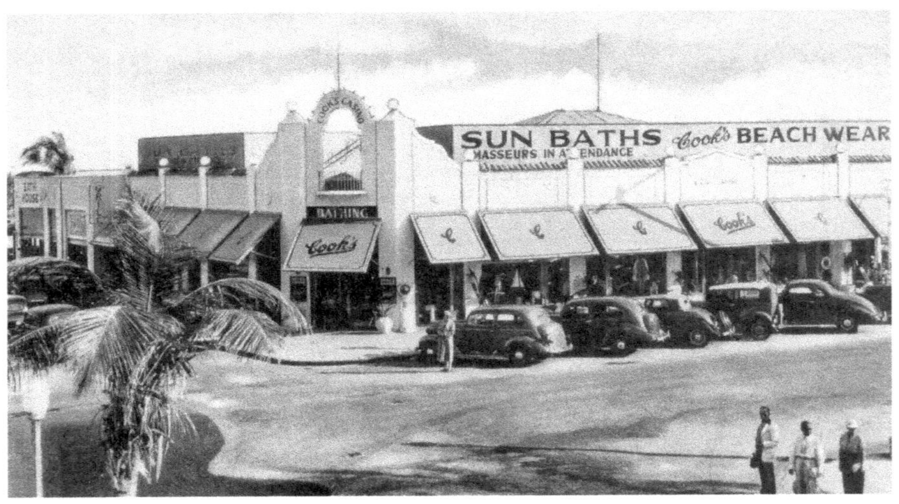

Cook's, built in 1926, was the fourth bathhouse in Miami Beach and stood until 1968. *Postcard courtesy of Larry Wiggins.*

his family, with sons John III and Walter, to Florida in 1918, settling first in Buena Vista and moving to Miami Beach in the 1920s. He bought a tract of oceanfront land from Lummus:

> *Cook built a vast casino at 475 Ocean Drive...Middlemass Construction Company put up a modern cement block structure, slightly Spanish in style. John Cook added crisp, striped awnings. He knew the beach customers preferred a gay, carnival spirit. He didn't want his casino to resemble a Spanish castle or an Italian palazzo.*[28]

The architect of Cook's Casino was probably William F. Brown, who had designed a store building for Cook on the same lot four months earlier. The casino was heavily damaged in the 1926 hurricane when a barge crashed into it, but it recovered and operated for many years thereafter, with John Cook III and his brother Walter as proprietors. In July 1968, Cook's Casino and Bathhouse were sold, to be replaced by apartments.[29]

Plans for an amusement pier at the foot of Biscayne Street got underway in 1925, and George R.K. Carter from Ohio began construction in early 1926. The hurricane that September carried much of it away. Another hurricane wrecked it again in 1928. Originally estimated to cost $480,000, it was soon called Carter's Million Dollar Pier. Carter sought help from sports promoter Tex Rickard from New York, who got the pier finished in 1929 and at the same time built the dog track nearby. William F. Brown is credited with designing the pier.

The pier reached 570 feet out into the ocean, and its amenities included a dance pavilion, a stage theater, a shooting gallery and a bar. In the 1930s, it was the venue for Minsky's Burlesque. In 1940, the city council purchased both the pier and Hardie's Casino, intending to put in a park. But two years later, the pier achieved a greater purpose during World War II, when Miami Beach became a major training center for the U.S. Army Air Forces. All over the city, hotels were converted to barracks, restaurants became mess halls, theaters were used as classrooms and the beach and golf courses were drill fields. General Henry H. Arnold said early in January 1944 that the war effort would have been set back by six to eight months if the Miami Beach hotels had not been available and a training center had to be built.

The city council, which owned the pier at that time, donated it as a recreation center for the trainees, and it came to be called the Servicemen's Pier. It was staffed by hundreds of volunteers, mostly women, from the community. Architect Russell Pancoast's wife Katherine, or Kay, headed the committee. Starting in April 1942, the pier provided a vital service in boosting

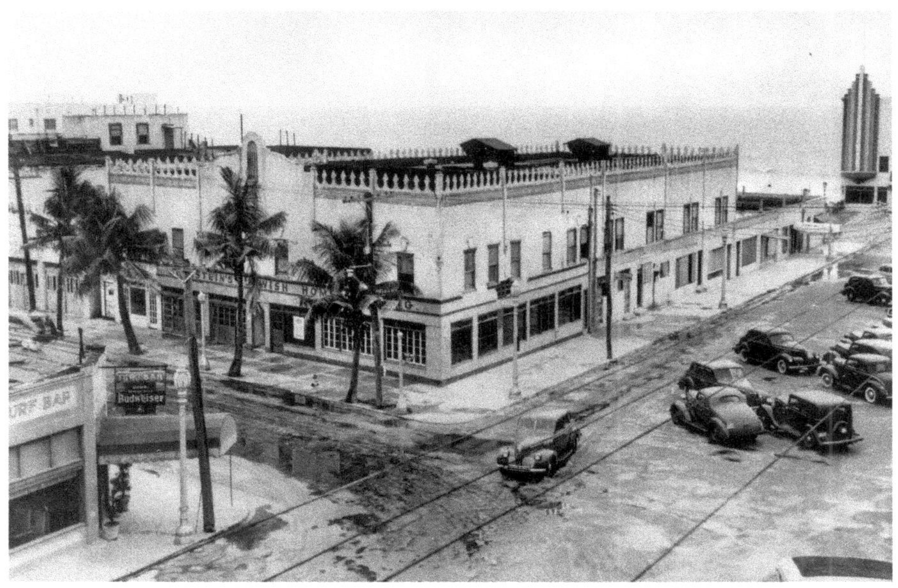

Bernstein's Jewish Home Cooking, 1930s, on Ocean Drive at Biscayne Street. The "Million Dollar Pier" is at far right. *Courtesy Arva Moore Parks.*

morale with dances, movies, swimming facilities, a library, a canteen and entertainment, and the navy used it for part of its training program. This extraordinary effort was a great success, serving 235,000 troops in its first year alone.[30] After this illustrious past, the Municipal Pier was demolished in 1985.

On the site of the old Ocean Beach Realty office, where Miami Beach had been founded in 1915, William F. Brown designed a new building in 1929. This was another project of George R.K. Carter, who had built the pier a block away. It was a two-story commercial structure embellished with a fancy roof. In this strongly Jewish neighborhood, in the 1930s, Esther Bernstein had a restaurant here that advertised "Jewish Home Cooking," as seen in the accompanying photo. This building on the old Lummus office site was demolished in 1941. J.N. Lummus himself swung the first sledgehammer.[31]

Chapter 3

The Miami Beach Improvement Company

John Stiles Collins (1837–1928) had invested in the coconut plantation project of Field, Osborn and Lum. Like them, Collins was from New Jersey, from Moorestown, near Philadelphia. He was a Quaker, an expert horticulturist and a frugal businessman:

> *The nursery business he conducted at Moorestown was on a large farm handed down through five generations. He had added much to it. Mr. Collins started in the coconut business here with six associates, and 334,000 trees were planted here in the winters of 1882, 1883, and 1884. At that time the pioneer, in middle age, came here because he could not stand cold weather.*[32]

Collins and his wife, Rachel, first spent the winters in Hypoluxo, on Lake Worth in Palm Beach County. They had five children, who kept the family business going up north: sons Irving, Arthur J. and Lester and daughters Mary and Katherine. Katherine was married to Thomas Pancoast (a variation of the British surname Panckhurst), who was also a Quaker. For twenty-four years, Collins and his son-in-law operated the Collins & Pancoast building supplies company in Merchantville, New Jersey.

> [The coconut project] *ended in failure and the stockholders dropped out, leaving only Mr. Collins and Elnathan T. Field. A former fruit grower and nurseryman, Mr. Collins could not see the land lie idle so bought Field's share of 1600 acres at Miami Beach and in 1905 started*

> [planting] *165 acres of avocados, including 7,000 trees. He also planted 500 Hayden mangoes.*[33]

While engaged in this operation, Collins and his wife stayed at a hotel in Miami, and Collins would cross Biscayne Bay to his farmland by boat. His land extended from present-day Fourteenth Street to around Sixty-seventh Street, but the farm was on the west bank of Indian Creek north of Twenty-third Street.

Collins's family came south to check up on their patriarch and saw the potential for developing a winter resort here comparable to Atlantic City in their home state, which had become popular by that time. The Collins-Pancoast family formed the Miami Beach Improvement Company on June 3, 1912, for that purpose. This appears to be the earliest official use of the name "Miami Beach." The company was always entirely family run and never sold shares. Collins was its president for life.

But Collins was still devoted to farming. One problem he had was getting his crops to the port and railroad in Miami for shipment north; mangrove swamp lined the bay, and parts of the bay itself were too shallow to navigate. His solution was to dredge a canal, still called the Collins Canal, from the terminus of Indian Creek southwesterly to the bay. The canal was finished in November 1912. At the same time, Collins had started building the two-and-a-half-mile Collins Bridge as the first causeway across Biscayne Bay, but then he ran out of money.

At this point, Carl Graham Fisher (1874–1939) enters the story. Fisher was from Indianapolis, where he and his business partner, James Allison, had made a fortune with their Prest-O-Lite company that manufactured gas-powered automobile headlights. What had made them the fortune was selling the patent to the Union Carbide Company for millions of dollars. Fisher had also, with Allison as an investor, built the Indianapolis Speedway and instituted its classic race. Fisher and his wife, Jane, had settled in Miami for the winters when he happened upon the Collins Bridge project: "Mr. Collins was 74 years old when he started the bridge, and Mr. Fisher said if a man of his age had that much vision and courage he deserved help. Mr. Fisher loaned $50,000 toward the bridge project."[34]

The bridge was completed in 1913. Built of Dade County pine from the mainland, it was the longest wooden bridge in the world at the time and the first link between the city of Miami and the beach. In exchange for his help with the bridge, Collins gave Fisher a two-hundred-acre tract of land, from ocean to bay, between Fifteenth and Nineteenth Streets. We will see what Fisher did with that in Chapter 8.

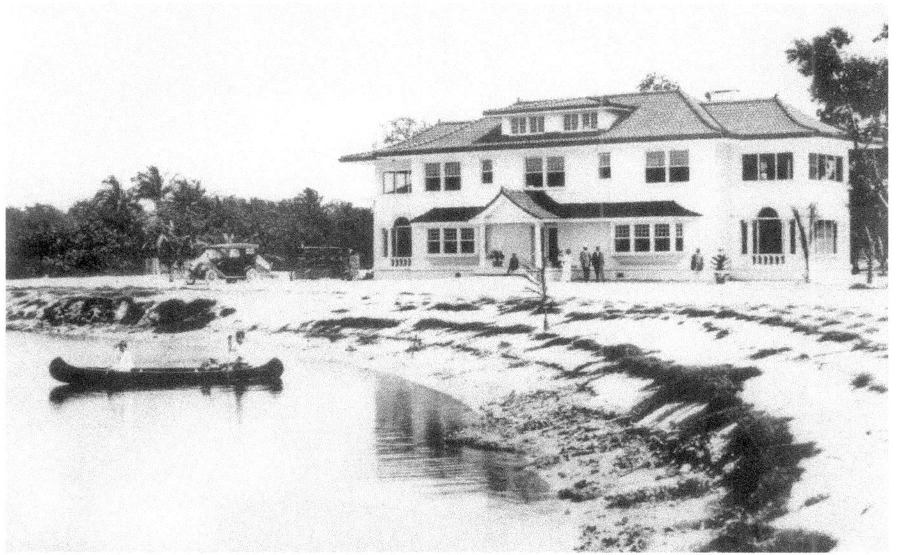

Thomas J. Pancoast and family built their house on Lake Pancoast in 1914. *Courtesy Arva Moore Parks.*

Collins had constructed the canal and bridge to aid his farming efforts, but they also literally paved the way for further development of the beach, allowing building materials and equipment to be brought in. At the east end of the canal, where it met Indian Creek, the shallow basin was scooped out and bulkheaded to create Lake Pancoast. The Collins-Pancoast family left a lasting mark on the beach with these engineering projects—we still have the Collins Canal and Lake Pancoast—but none of their buildings remain. These included the family's own homes, their public bathhouse and their grand hotel on the ocean.

Thomas Pancoast had moved here to assist Collins while the rest of the family returned to New Jersey. Pancoast would become a prominent citizen in Miami Beach and served as the city's second mayor. In 1914, Pancoast built a graceful, two-story home for his family on the north shore of the lake. It was designed by architect John W. King and was the first house in the area to be built of poured concrete. Thomas and Katherine Pancoast had sons Norman, Russell and J. Arthur Pancoast (not to be confused with his uncle, Arthur J. Collins). Russell Pancoast would later be a notable Miami Beach architect after graduating from Cornell in 1922. The Pancoast house was demolished in 1953 after standing less than forty years.

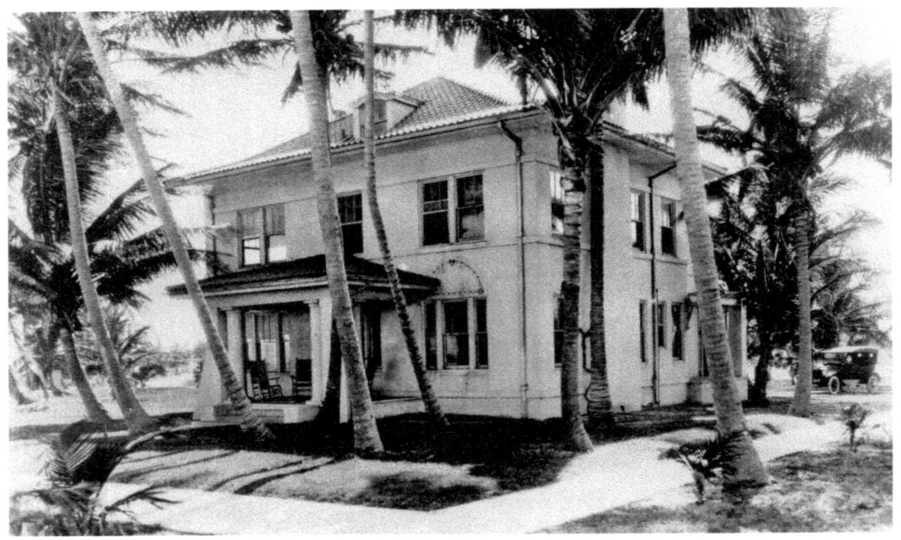

Home of Miami Beach pioneer John S. Collins, built in 1914 on the ocean at Twenty-fifth Street. *Courtesy City of Miami Beach Historical Archive.*

John Collins also built his more modest two-story home in 1914, on the east side of Lake Pancoast, facing the ocean. It was just at this time that Collins was widowed; his first wife, Rachel, "died in 1914, at the time he was completing his oceanfront residence. He married in 1916 Mrs. Ida P. Horner of Merchantville (New Jersey)"[35] when he was seventy-eight.

Also in 1914, the Pancoasts opened the Miami Beach Casino on the ocean at Twenty-third Street. It was the third bathhouse on the beach, after Smith's and Hardie's farther south:

> *The Miami Beach Improvement Company built a third casino, which was the first on the beach to have a swimming pool. It was opened as The Miami Beach Bathing Pavilion and Swimming Pool and shortly changed to the Miami Beach Casino. Funds were none too ample at the time and a number of salvaged timbers from wrecked ships were used in the framework of the building. Its exterior was sheathed with shingles. Later Smith added a pool to his casino facilities and Hardie followed suit.*[36]

In 1916, Carl Fisher bought the Miami Beach Casino, which was rather rustic, and gave it a lavish makeover. He renamed it the Roman Pools to make it more exotic and added a second swimming pool, parallel to the first.[37] Fisher

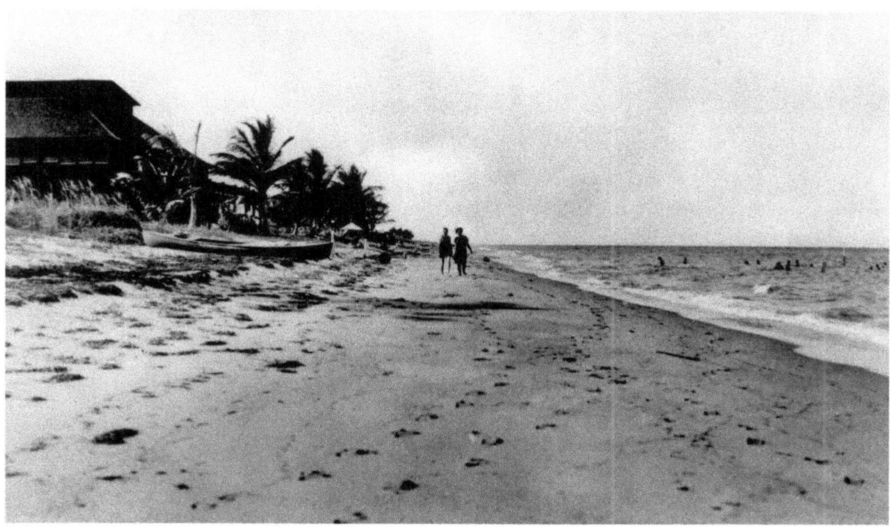

The Miami Beach Bathing Pavilion in 1915. Carl Fisher later remodeled it as the Roman Pools. *Courtesy City of Miami Beach Historical Archive.*

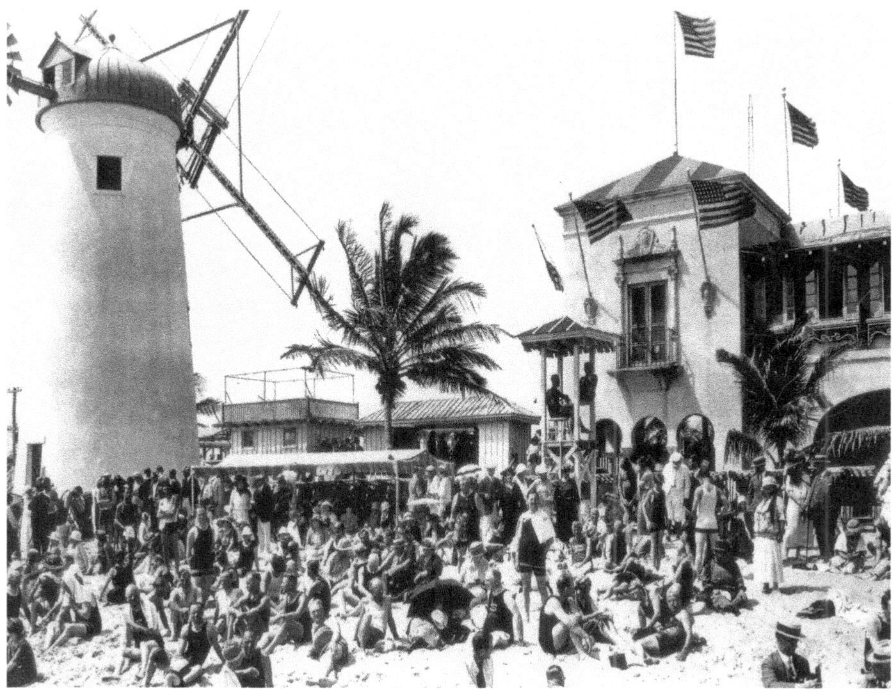

The Roman Pools and its famous windmill, on the beach at Twenty-third Street. *Courtesy Arva Moore Parks,* Miami News *collection.*

brought in C.J. Wacker, a contractor from Indianapolis, to construct a distinctive windmill that served as a pump to fill the pools with seawater. The windmill was forty feet high, twenty-two feet in diameter and had a nine-thousand-gallon holding tank. August Geiger was supervising architect for Fisher's work on the Roman Pools,[38] but Martin Hampton may have had a hand in it, based on a rendering signed by him.[39] There were two buildings facing Twenty-third Street, the Baths on the west and the Casino to the east. Each building had two domed pinnacles and elaborate Beaux-Arts ornamentation.

The Roman Pools often had entertainment and exhibition diving, and it was one of the town's most popular gathering places. On Wednesday evening, February 6, 1918, the Casino was the scene of a grand "Allies Ball."[40] More than two hundred people attended in costumes of the many nations allied against Germany in World War I. The war had started in Europe in August 1914, and the United States entered the conflict in April 1917. This gala was held less than a year later and was hosted by Mr. and Mrs. John Hanan, who lived next door to Carl Fisher at the east end of Lincoln Road. There is no record that Carl attended the party, but his wife, Jane, came in a Japanese kimono, and Mrs. Hanan wore peacock feathers as an Egyptian grandee. Mrs. Bethel Tatum came as Brittania. James Snowden represented Belgium.

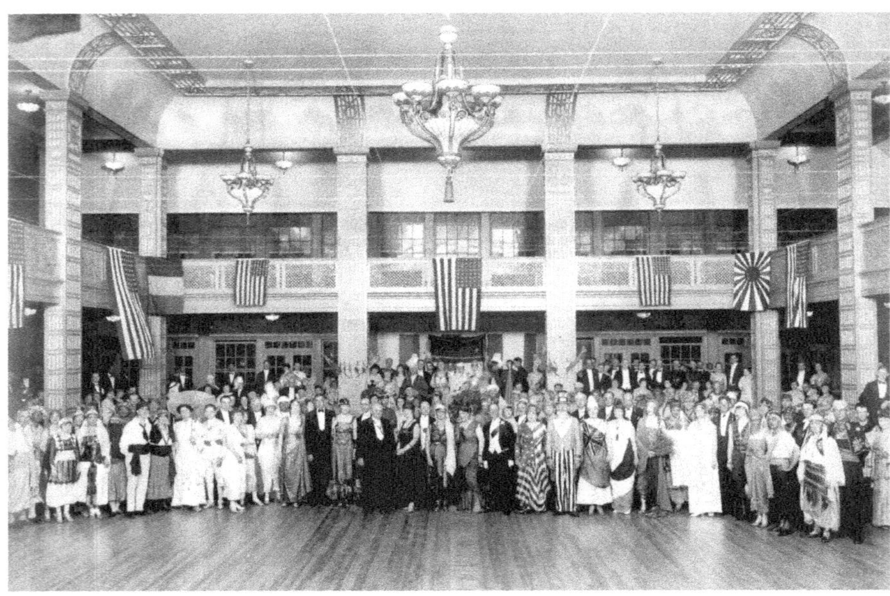

The Allies Ball at the Roman Pools in 1918, with guests in the costumes of the allied nations in World War I. *Courtesy City of Miami Beach Historical Archive.*

The Pancoasts remained Americans, and architect August Geiger's wife was a Persian princess. Miami Beach mayor J.N. Lummus apparently did not attend, but Miami mayor Everest G. Sewell, dressed as Uncle Sam, led the ceremonies together with his wife as Columbia (the female counterpart of Uncle Sam, not the country of Colombia). The reception began at nine thirty. The costumed guests, many carrying flags, paraded before the Sewells to trumpet fanfare and orchestral music, and a supper was served at ten thirty. When the war ended with the Armistice in November, Mayor Sewell put on his Uncle Sam outfit again for the celebrations in Miami.

The Snowden Estate

On April 6, 1916, James H. Snowden purchased 1,600 feet of the oceanfront, plus an additional tract on the other side of Indian Creek, from the Miami Beach Improvement Company.[41] Snowden, born in Pennsylvania in 1875, had made his fortune in oil. He hired architect Herbert Bass and Company of Indianapolis to design a winter estate that was the finest building Miami Beach would see for quite some time. It

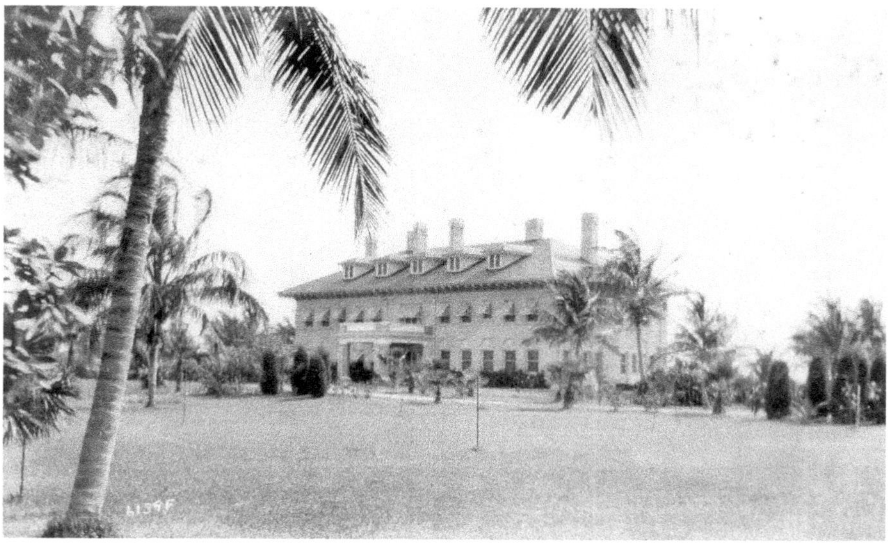

The west façade of the James Snowden estate, built in 1916 on the ocean at Forty-fourth Street. *Courtesy Arva Moore Parks, Pete Chase collection.*

was probably James Allison, Carl Fisher's partner in Prest-O-Lite, who referred Snowden to the Bass Company. A few years earlier (1911–14), Bass had designed a "country estate" for Allison in Indianapolis. Allison had Bass design the building itself but hired Philadelphia architects Price & McLanahan to do the interior.[42] Allison's home became the campus of Marian College in 1937.

This, too, was a "country estate" in a rugged setting at the northern limits of the new town. Its construction at that time and place was astounding. In ten years, it would be the premier house on Miami Beach's "Millionaires' Row," which is the subject of another chapter, but it deserves separate treatment here because it was built so much earlier and was such a coup for the Collins company.

The house, of two stories plus an attic, was a stately, symmetrical structure in the Renaissance style. It had a hip roof with dormers, lunettes over the windows and a round-arched loggia overlooking the sea. There were several outbuildings, and the extensive grounds were landscaped. Inside, the floor plan provided cross ventilation, and the rooms were sumptuously furnished. The house itself was valued at $60,000, but its complete furnishings and landscaping doubled this sum.

The Snowden house was written up in the September 1917 issue of *Architecture and Building*:

> *In the decorative treatment, English motifs predominate with certain divergencies* [sic] *in the French and Renaissance periods. From the vestibule paneled in Istrian marble into the central hall the tones of the sea predominate. The hall is wainscoted in oblong oak panels...The dining room is in Louis XVI style, paneled to the ceiling with hand rubbed tinting in gold and silver tone.*[43]

The dining room ceiling had been salvaged from a building by Stanford White. One can only wonder if it was conveyed here down the Collins Canal.

The house had its grand opening on March 29, 1917. The Snowdens hosted a reception with dinner and dancing, with rainbow lanterns lighting the path to the sea.[44] This was only a few months after industrialist James Deering's Miami estate, Villa Vizcaya, another Renaissance palace in the wilderness, opened on Christmas Day 1916.

Tire magnate Harvey Firestone bought Snowden's estate in 1923, and it became better known as the Firestone Estate. Firestone was experimenting with new plant sources of latex on the tract of land across Indian Creek

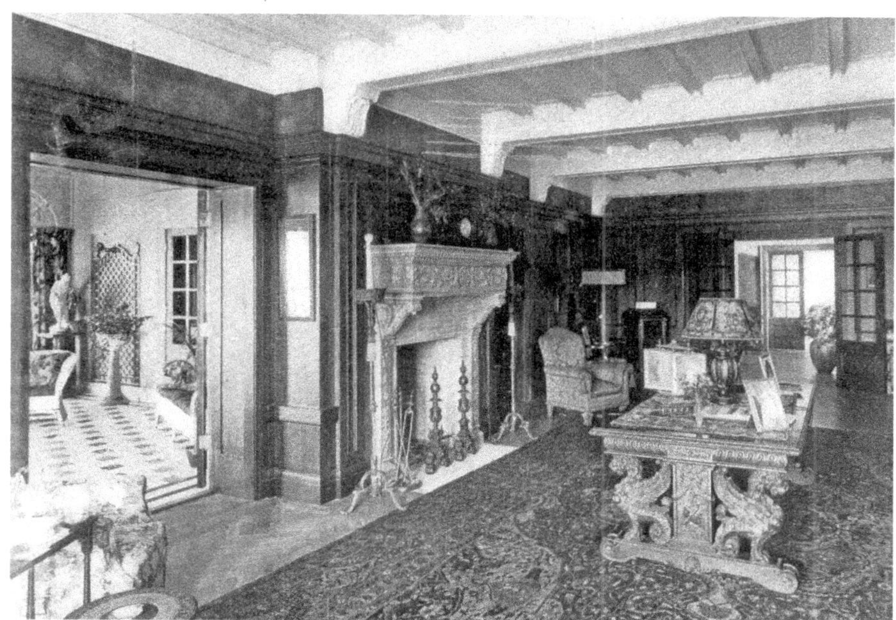

Living room and loggia of the Snowden estate. It is easy to see how refreshing the smooth simplicity of Art Deco would be a few years later. *From* Architecture and Building, *September 1917, courtesy Arva Moore Parks.*

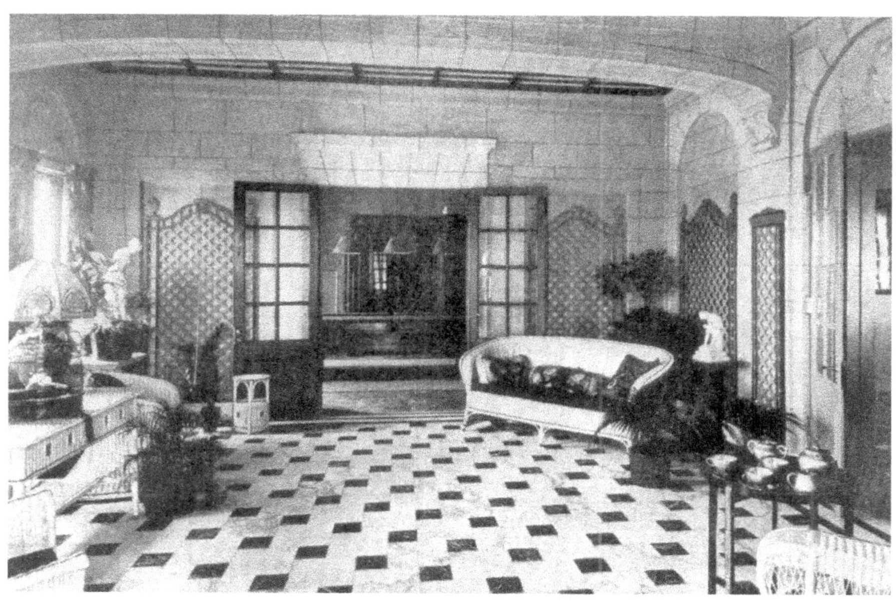

from the mansion. Thomas Edison, who was conducting similar research at his winter home in Fort Myers, often visited his friend Firestone and his "experimental rubber garden" on Pine Tree Drive to compare notes.[45]

Harvey Firestone Sr. died in 1938. During World War II, when Miami Beach became a major military training center, the Firestone mansion served as quite luxurious officers' quarters. In 1954, as you may know, the Fontainebleau Hotel was built beside the Firestone mansion, which served as construction headquarters before it was torn down. Fontainebleau architect Morris Lapidus spent many days there. Could that black-and-white marble floor of the loggia, assuming it had survived nearly forty years, have inspired Lapidus's famous bow-ties in the floor of the Fontainebleau lobby?

Early Hotels

Fulfilling the Collins family's goal of creating a resort, hotels soon appeared in their territory. Immediately to the south of John Collins's house, the Breakers Hotel opened in 1917 as the third hotel in the new town of Miami Beach, following Brown's Hotel on Ocean Drive and Carl Fisher's Lincoln Hotel on Lincoln Road. The Breakers offered two-room apartments with kitchenettes, right on the ocean. Cora Wofford was leasing it and charged guests the exorbitant rate of $25 a day (comparable

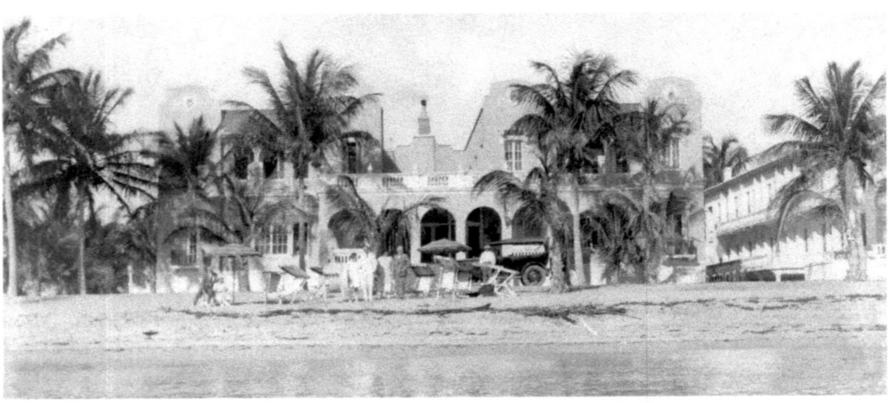

From left to right: The Wofford and Breakers Hotels, two of the earliest in Miami Beach, on the ocean at Twenty-fourth Street. *Courtesy Arva Moore Parks, Pete Chase collection.*

to $465 in 2014).[46] Four years later, the Woffords built their own fifty-room Wofford Hotel next door to it, which "became one of the leading resort hotels of the Beach."[47]

In 1919, Collins's grandson J. Arthur Pancoast had built a small house for himself on the ocean at Twenty-ninth Street. There were still no grand oceanfront hotels at that time, so Arthur moved his house in order to place his Pancoast Hotel on that prime spot. The house was taken three blocks away, to 2633 Indian Creek Drive, but it was demolished in 1952. The Pancoast Hotel, which opened in January 1924, was designed by architect Martin L. Hampton and is discussed further in Chapter 10. The Pancoast served as a military hospital during World War II and was demolished in 1953 for the construction of the Seville Hotel.

The Mediterranean Style

Buildings such as the Pancoast Hotel, with their barrel-tile roofs and round-arched arcades, are usually described as Mediterranean Revival style, but this is actually a misnomer, and there is a campaign afoot to correct it. The architectural style of choice in the 1920s in both Florida and California was invented to evoke the atmosphere of Old Spain or Italy, but there was no former "Mediterranean" style that was being brought back. The new style was a product of its own time, when architects would tour southern Europe and northern Africa and bring back sketches of the buildings there. They would take disparate elements from various architectural traditions and reassemble them to suit their clients and to adapt to modern needs. The style was seen as romantic and exotic. It was also desirable to create the illusion of age in these brand-new buildings, which was sometimes achieved by beating the walls with chains, cultivating moss and importing centuries-old clay roof tiles, with their patina, from old Spanish colonial buildings.

Coral Gables architect H. George Fink was one who made the tour, and in his writings in 1923, he coined the term "Mediterranean" to describe this newly devised style. The word "Revival" erroneously became attached to the term some years later. This is how Fink explained the style:

> *From the Spanish and Italian we derive the cool, inviting loggias, the large and attractive patios, the terraces that are a delight in the evening and late afternoons, and the grills and ornamental stone doorways. From the*

Moorish and Persian we obtain the delightful effects from using colored and glazed tile for inserts, wrought iron lanterns, ornate columns and other unique treatments too numerous to enumerate. But the one feature common to all which we have retained in all the houses are the delightfully varied tile roofs and the tile floors. The gaily colored awnings are also one of the notes of color that are so prevalent in all types.[48]

LOOKING AHEAD

Near the shore at Twenty-third Street, a "Marconi wireless station," consisting of two tall radio towers, was "put up in 1914 as part of the government's first attempts at ship-to-shore communication."[49] The view looking south from one of these towers in 1919 shows the south portion of the Miami Beach Improvement Company's land and Fisher's tract just beyond it, where he was beginning to develop Lincoln Road.

For years, the Collins-Pancoast family reserved the huge oceanfront lot between Twenty-third and Twenty-fourth Streets for a grand hotel, but potential investors felt the site was too far north. What developer Newton

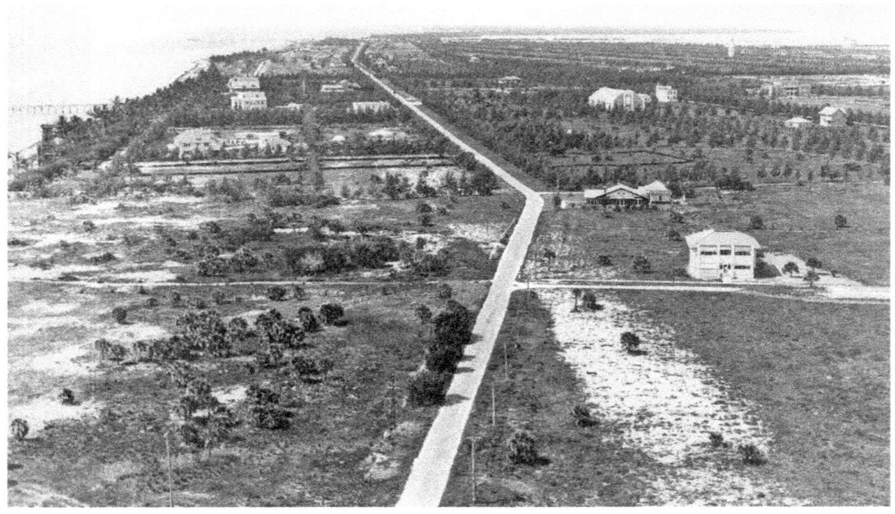

Looking south from the Marconi radio tower at Twenty-third Street in 1919. Collins Avenue is at center, the El Mar Apartments at right and Lincoln Road in the distance. *Courtesy City of Miami Beach Historical Archive.*

B.T. Roney eventually built there in 1925 became the crown jewel of this neighborhood and, indeed, of the entire city: the Roney Plaza Hotel. More on that in Chapter 10.

Six weeks after his ninetieth birthday, John Collins died at his oceanfront home on February 10, 1928. He had been out to inspect the city's bulkheading of the beach by his house the previous month and never regained his strength, but he continued watching the project from his bed. His funeral was an unstructured Quaker service at the house. The *Miami Herald* wrote him this tribute:

> *Mr. Collins loved Miami Beach in all its parts and seldom left it after he came here to reside. He loved the outdoors, and his long life was undoubtedly due to the fact that he lived the last half of his life in a warm climate. From the time he first saw Miami Beach his best efforts were given in its development. He saw all his dreams come true.*[50]

CHAPTER 4

FIFTH STREET

Miami Beach got its second link to Miami when the County Causeway opened on February 17, 1920. (It was renamed for General Douglas MacArthur in 1942.) It ran along the north side of the Government Cut shipping channel and entered Miami Beach at Fifth Street, which then became a major thoroughfare. Carl Fisher, though, had started building on Fifth Street as early as 1916 in anticipation of the causeway. He also constructed an electric plant for Miami Beach on Peninsular Terminal Island, a spoil bank just offshore. Before that, Miami Beach got its electricity from a plant in Miami, but service was sporadic and expensive.

World War I delayed the causeway construction. A few years before its completion, the first building to go up on Fifth Street was the office of Fisher's own realty company.

THE MIAMI OCEAN VIEW COMPANY

In April 1916, the Lummus brothers, in financial straits, joined with Carl Fisher and others to form the Miami Ocean View Realty Company. The others included Fisher's Prest-O-Lite partner, James Allison, and oilman James Snowden, who was soon to build his oceanfront mansion. The company took over the former Lummus land west of Washington Avenue and north of Fifth Street. The accompanying photograph looking eastward

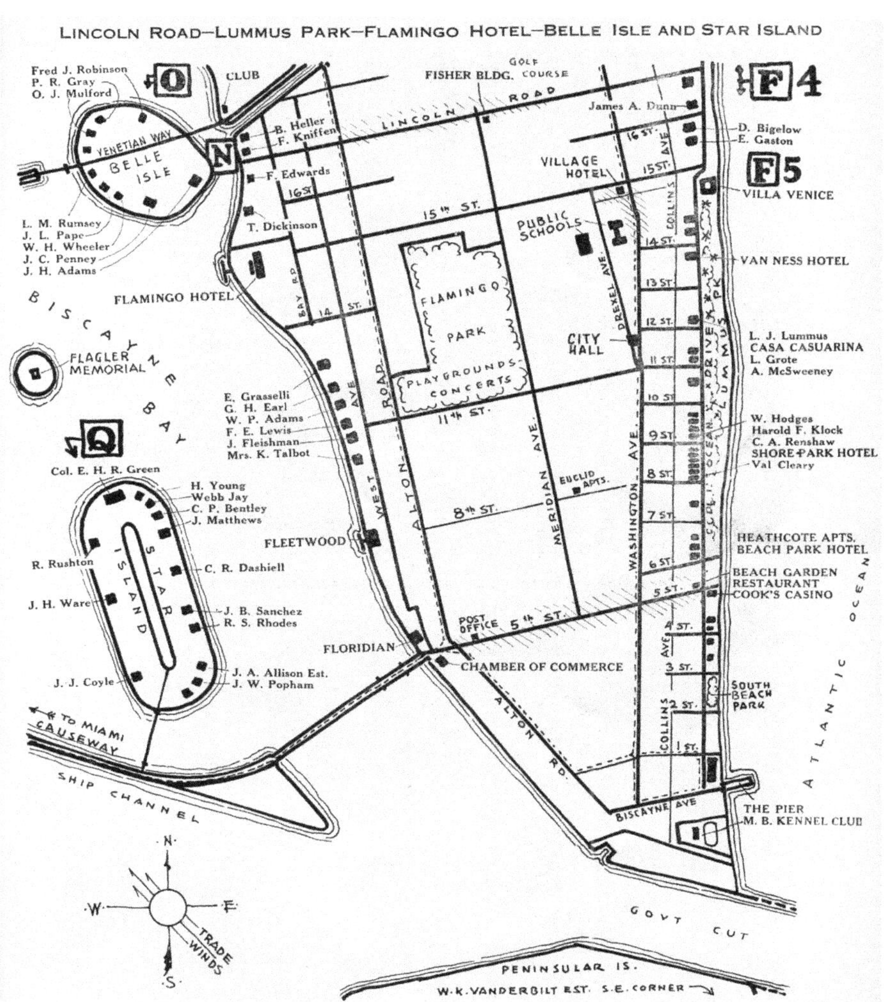

Map of Miami Beach south of Lincoln Road, published by Frank F. Stearns in 1932. *Courtesy Arva Moore Parks.*

down Fifth Street in 1921 shows several buildings on the north side, developed by Fisher's company, but none at all on the south side that was still Lummus territory. The south side of Fifth Street never fared well; when the street was widened in 1974, the small commercial buildings that then lined the south side were obliterated.

The Miami Ocean View Realty Company's own office was a two-story Beaux-Arts structure at 1145 Fifth Street. It appears in the Sanborn Fire

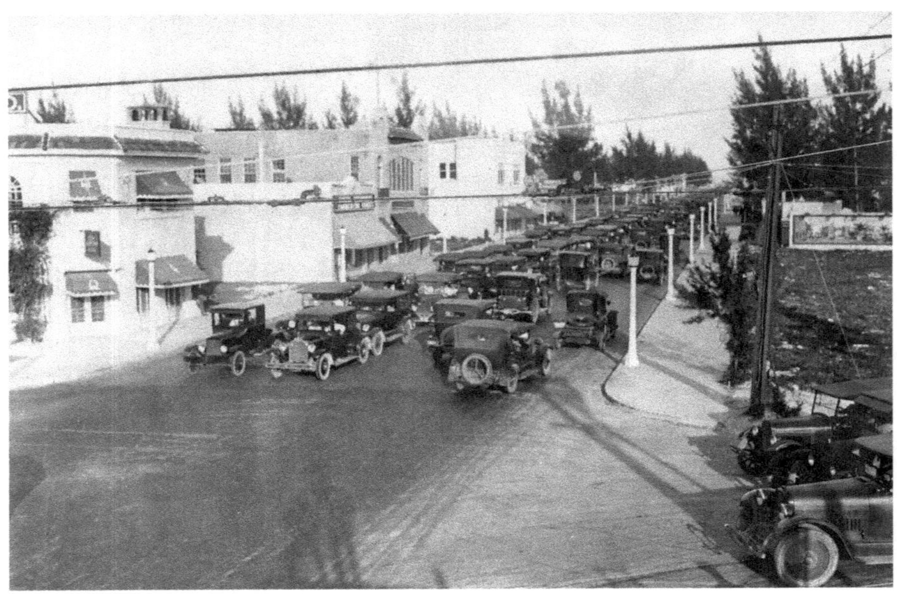

Street scene at the foot of the County Causeway, Alton Road and Fifth Street, 1921. The Miami Ocean View Realty office is at left, and the post office is at center. *Courtesy City of Miami Beach Historical Archive.*

Insurance map of March 1918 and was very likely designed by Fisher's favorite architect, August Geiger. It was demolished in the 1940s for the construction of a gas station.

In the 1920s, Fisher made this stretch of Fifth Street the civic, commercial and communication center of the new city of Miami Beach. Soon, it would be the site of the post office, a telegraph office, the chamber of commerce, a trolley line, several hotels and a novel tourist attraction.

MIAMI BEACH AQUARIUM

To the west of the realty office, on the bay front just north of the new causeway, Fisher's Indianapolis business partner, James Allison, constructed a public aquarium that opened on January 1, 1921. Besides being a tourist attraction, it was also a respected scientific institution, with over fifty exhibition tanks. It was also famously where Allison's stash of liquor was found on a raid during Prohibition.

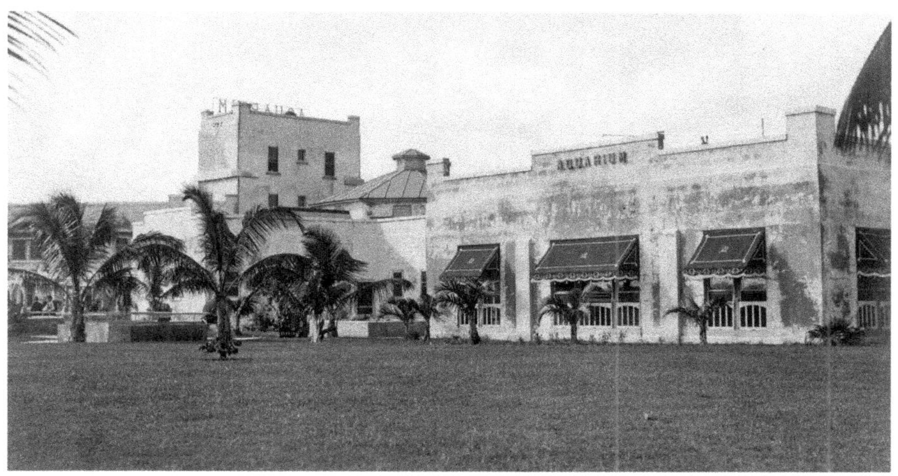

James Allison's Miami Beach Aquarium at Alton Road and Fifth Street. *Postcard courtesy of Larry Wiggins.*

Every fall, Captain Charley Thompson would stock the aquarium's coral rock–lined pools with his ocean finds: porgies, grunts, pork fish, amberjack, barracuda, moray eels, crabs, sea anemones and even sand dollars. At the end of the tourist season, the specimens would be released back into the sea. The aquarium was open daily from 10:00 a.m. to 6:00 p.m. Admission was fifty cents for adults and twenty-five cents for children. But the aquarium was short-lived; after only four years, Allison sold the building and grounds to Jerome Cherbino, who tore down the Miami Beach Aquarium in 1925 to build the Floridian Hotel slightly north of its site. There is more about the Floridian in Chapter 10.

THE CHAMBER OF COMMERCE AND TROLLEYS

On the south side of Fifth Street across from the aquarium, the Miami Beach Chamber of Commerce built its first office in January 1922. The chamber had been organized on July 22, 1921, at a meeting of prominent citizens at Smith's Casino. Thomas Pancoast was elected president. Within two months, it had 305 members, almost half the city's resident population:

> *Most of the early meetings were held either at Smith's or Hardie's Casino, but the Chamber's first place of business was under a beach umbrella at the*

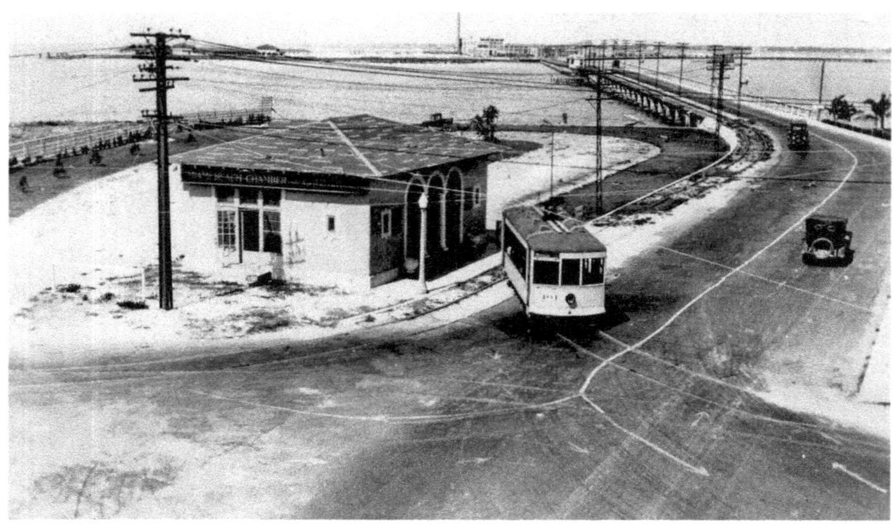

The chamber of commerce building and trolley line at the foot of the County Causeway. *Courtesy City of Miami Beach Historical Archive.*

> *corner of Fifth Street and Alton Road...one of the most strategic locations in the city.*[51]

This location, at the eastbound end of the new County Causeway, was ideal for the chamber to greet arriving visitors. In December 1921, the chamber raised funds to build this charming Beaux-Arts building there as its information bureau and headquarters. Among the chamber's early projects for the city were paved streets and sidewalks, a boardwalk, lighting on the causeway, a potable water supply, parks and enlarging the school. It also brought Miami Beach its first bank, First National, on Lincoln Road.

With the causeway, Miami Beach also got a trolley line. At first, it was operated by Carl Fisher's Miami Beach Electric Company. It started service on December 18, 1920, with ten cars on a route that started in downtown Miami. The causeway had a drawbridge in those days, where an elaborate steel structure kept the overhead trolley wire aligned. From the end of the causeway at Alton Road and Fifth Street, the trolleys took a bi-directional circular route: down Alton Road to First Street, east to Washington Avenue (then called Miami Avenue), north to Nineteenth Street, east to Park Avenue (then called Sheridan Avenue), north to Twenty-third Street, across the Collins Canal bridge, west on Dade Boulevard to Alton Road and then south back to Fifth Street.

In 1923, the trolley service split off from the electric company and incorporated as the Miami Beach Railway Company. In March 1924, American Power and Light took over both the trolley and the electric plant and the next year turned them over to Florida Power and Light. In the winter season of 1924–25, the trolley system got twelve new, larger cars, but the circular route was abandoned, and the trolleys ran on two separate lines. One went up Washington, Park and Sheridan Avenues and Pine Tree Drive to Fifty-first Street, but this line did poorly and closed in July 1927. The other route went up Alton Road to Forty-fifth Street. It served the Nautilus Hotel and polo grounds and the Garden Theatre and lasted until July 1933. The Railway Company began replacing trolley cars with buses on its various routes starting in 1927. Finally, the trolleys just had a short loop from the causeway down to the casinos and movie theater at Biscayne Street. Trolley service at Miami Beach ended on October 17, 1939.[52]

THE FIRST POST OFFICE

When Miami Beach became a town in 1915, it began to get mail delivery by courier from Miami via the Collins Bridge. Fisher saw that Miami Beach needed its own post office, but he saved the government the trouble of building

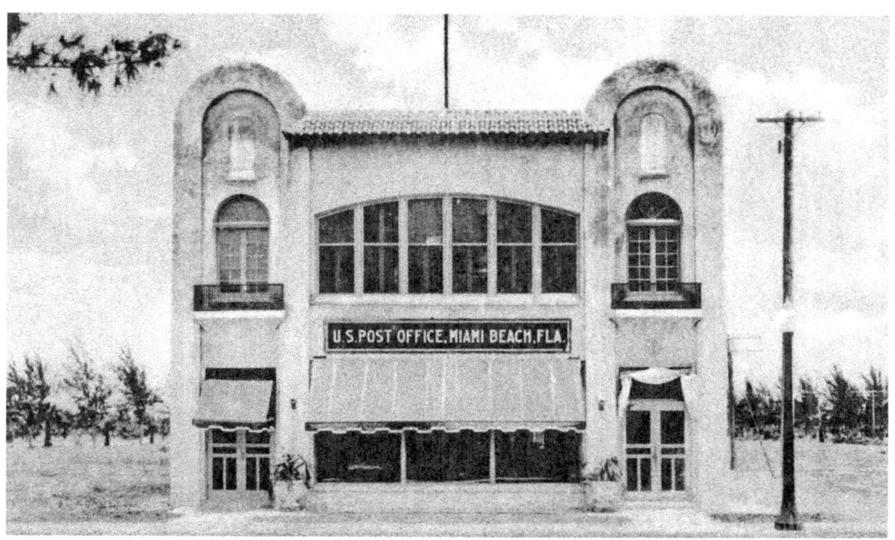

Miami Beach's first post office, built on Fifth Street in 1920. *Postcard courtesy of Larry Wiggins.*

one—and got one sooner—by having the Miami Ocean View Company build it. They not only built it but also furnished it and kept it stocked with office supplies.[53] This post office, the city's first, opened on December 1, 1920, with a staff of four. A two-story building of masonry vernacular style, its front façade had expansive arched windows between two full-height rounded arches. The post office operated here until it moved into larger quarters at 1015 Washington Avenue in 1933, at which time this building became the Reilly Hotel, owned by Robert Reilly. The second-story office space was used by the Miami Ocean View Company as a boardroom—the company had, after all, built this building—and its long mahogany table remained there until the building was demolished in 1997.

Just west of the post office, the Miami Ocean View Company had also built and furnished a little one-story Postal Telegraph office in 1923. It was demolished in 1987.

Commercial Buildings

Next door to the post office on the east was the Fitch Building, built in 1921. The Lamont Laundry was one of its early tenants. Architects for this two-story commercial building were Martin L. Hampton and Robert R. Reimert, Hampton's associate at the time. Next door to the Fitch Building, which was demolished in 1973, the Causeway Pharmacy opened in 1921 at the corner of Lenox Avenue. Escaping demolition, it was restored and incorporated into new construction on the site. It is one of the two surviving 1920s buildings on Fifth Street; the other, also built in 1921, is a few blocks east, at 821 Fifth Street. It was originally the Beach Haven Hotel and is now a restaurant.

A block east of the Causeway Pharmacy, at the corner of Michigan Avenue, the Prince George Hotel was built late in 1925. This three-story building contained both apartments and retail space and cost $150,000 to build. The apartments had cooking facilities, and summer rates in 1928 were $50 to $100 per month. The Prince George was torn down in 1974. A block farther east at Jefferson Avenue was a popular one-story "refreshment stand" called the Pig Trail Inn that sprawled in a zigzag across two lots. Built in 1928, with George Bruce as architect, it became a gas station in 1950 and was demolished in 1989.

Western Union

At the corner of Meridian Avenue, next door to the Beach Haven Hotel, a Western Union telegraph office was built in 1925, designed by Walter DeGarmo. We will meet DeGarmo many times in these pages; he designed some exquisite buildings, but sadly most of those in Miami Beach have disappeared. This was a little one- and two-story Mission-style structure with a small corner tower and barrel-tile trim. From its appearance, one would never guess this building's importance as a telecommunication center: in 1925, its cable line connected to Buenos Aires. As the newspaper reported, "Every cable message handled by the company from any part of the United States to the eastern part of South America will be transferred from land to sea lines here."[54] Of course, with time, cablegrams became outmoded. In its last days, the building became a pharmacy. Surviving for seventy years, it was torn down in 1995, shortly before this area was designated as the Ocean Beach historic district.

Haddon Hotel

Newton B.T. Roney (1883–1952) is best known for the Roney Plaza Hotel, which he built in 1925 on the beach at Twenty-third Street, but before that, Roney developed many other properties throughout the city. The New Jersey lawyer came to Miami Beach in 1918 and bought out the Lummus brothers' interest in the Miami Ocean View Company. He would go on to develop four blocks of lower Collins Avenue, would buy William Whitman's residential project on Espanola Way and convert it to the Spanish Village and, in 1925, would buy the east end of Lincoln Road from Carl Fisher.

Roney's first building, in 1922, was the Haddon Hotel at the northwest corner of Fifth Street and Collins Avenue. This, like nearly all of Roney's buildings, was designed by architect Robert A. Taylor (1885–1961) in classic Mediterranean style. The Haddon had a distinctive third-story octagonal tower at the corner, and it was "Miami Beach's only hotel with a roof garden."[55] It also had a number of storefronts. In 1925, Taylor extended the building all the way to Sixth Street, and two more stories were added in 1934. By the 1940s, its name had changed to the Oceanic Hotel, and it was one of the hundreds of Miami Beach hotels that served as barracks for World War II trainees. Its sixty-three rooms

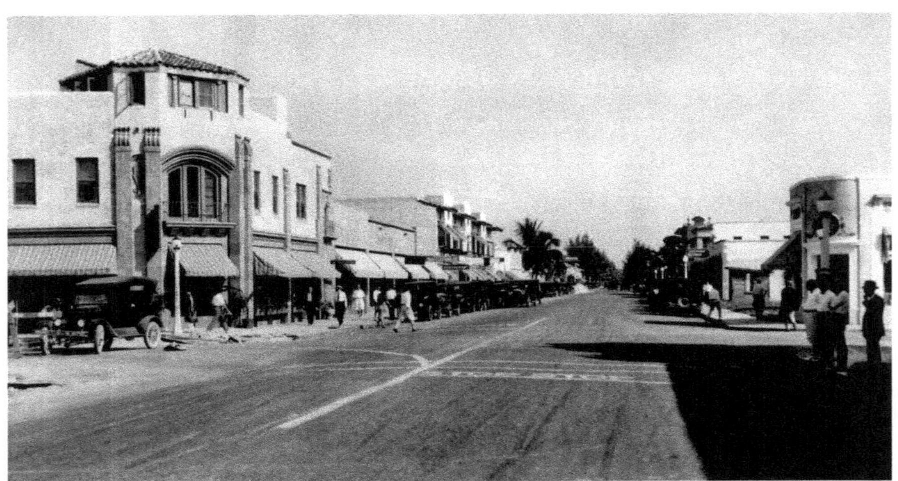

Looking north on Collins Avenue at Fifth Street in 1925. N.B.T. Roney's Haddon Hotel is at left, and the Standard Realty Company office is at right. *Courtesy City of Miami Beach Historical Archive.*

accommodated 254 men in bunk beds. It returned to civilian use in 1943 and was demolished in 1965.

One block east of the Haddon Hotel, we come to Cook's Casino, which we saw in Chapter 2, built in 1926 at Fifth Street and Ocean Drive.

Chapter 5
Ocean Drive

Whether or not you have been to Miami Beach, you are probably familiar with Ocean Drive. It originates at Biscayne Street (now called South Pointe Drive), south of where the numbered streets start, and runs northward along the beachfront for about a mile to Fifteenth Street. Its row of neon-lighted Depression-era hotels opposite Lummus Park is the signature streetscape of the city's Art Deco historic district and appears often in ads, movies and television shows. Many of the hotels here have been beautifully restored. But most of Ocean Drive itself has been lost. At one time, it was nearly twelve miles long.

The surviving portion of Ocean Drive dates back to the Lummus brothers' platting of the Ocean Beach Subdivision in 1912 and subsequent Ocean Beach Additions through 1914. In the early days, there were widely scattered residences here, including the homes of Miami Beach mayor Val Cleary at 800 Ocean Drive, longtime city manager Claude Renshaw at 844 and J.N. Lummus's own home, Salubrity, at 1204.

The first hotel in Miami Beach, still standing, opened in 1915 on Ocean Drive at First Street. A few years later, construction started for another hotel, the Strath Haven, at Fourth Street. It was the project of Martha Binder, who owned the Strath Haven Hotel in Atlantic City, New Jersey. She came to Miami Beach in 1917 and started to build a six-story hotel at 411 Ocean Drive in 1926, but then the boom collapsed. Architect William J. Brown completed the Strath Haven in 1929.[56] It was demolished forty years later.

Two generations of lost structures once stood on the east side of Ocean Drive at Fourteenth Street. First, Albert Bouche's Villa Venice, built at 1461 Ocean Drive in the 1920s, was a "restaurant theatre." It had tropical gardens, bathing facilities, music and a troupe of thirty-two performers. Bouche had another Villa Venice in a suburb of Chicago.[57] Unfortunately both were beset by mob activity, notably gambling. By 1939, this Villa Venice had moved to the Roman Pools building at Twenty-third Street, and the White House Hotel took its place on Ocean Drive.

The White House was a three-story hotel designed by architect Roy F. France—more on him in Chapter 10—in Neocolonial or Georgian style. This style evokes the architecture of early America, and it became especially popular after the nation's 150th birthday in 1926. Across Fifteenth Street, directly north of the White House, was Roy France's Jefferson Hotel, also built in 1939, but it was Art Deco in style and evoked early America in name only. By 1990, both the White House and the Jefferson were vacant and boarded up and subject to occasional arson fires. A conflagration at the Jefferson in October of that year resulted in both hotels being demolished as public hazards. The Betsy Ross Hotel still survives on Ocean Drive as the last remnant of this little Neocolonial enclave.

Carl Fisher's property, which he called Alton Beach, started at Fifteenth Street, and Ocean Drive continued to run through it until the 1930s. Fisher's own home at the east end of Lincoln Road had an Ocean Drive address. In the Miami Beach Improvement Company's property north of Nineteenth Street, the 1915 platting[58] shows the road as "Miami Beach Drive," and except for an interruption at the Twenty-third Street bathhouse, it extended up to Twenty-ninth Street. The Wofford and Breakers Hotels and John S. Collins's home all faced onto this oceanfront road. At Twenty-ninth Street, it turned west to join Collins Avenue. The Snowden estate, as we have seen, was built at Forty-fourth Street, at the north end of the city, in 1916.

The northern boundary of Miami Beach had been established at the town's founding in 1915 at approximately Forty-sixth Street. In September 1917, the Dade County Commission granted right of way for the Tatum brothers, realtors, to build an oceanfront road extending northward through unincorporated land, from the Miami Beach city limits to the coast adjacent to Fulford (163rd Street), in order to provide access to their landholdings there. This was the road that L.F. Tuten, keeper of the house of refuge, said "was built soon after I took charge in 1917." Like the roadway farther to the south, it was also called "Ocean Drive," and it stretched for more than seven miles along the deserted surf line north of Miami Beach. It became "one

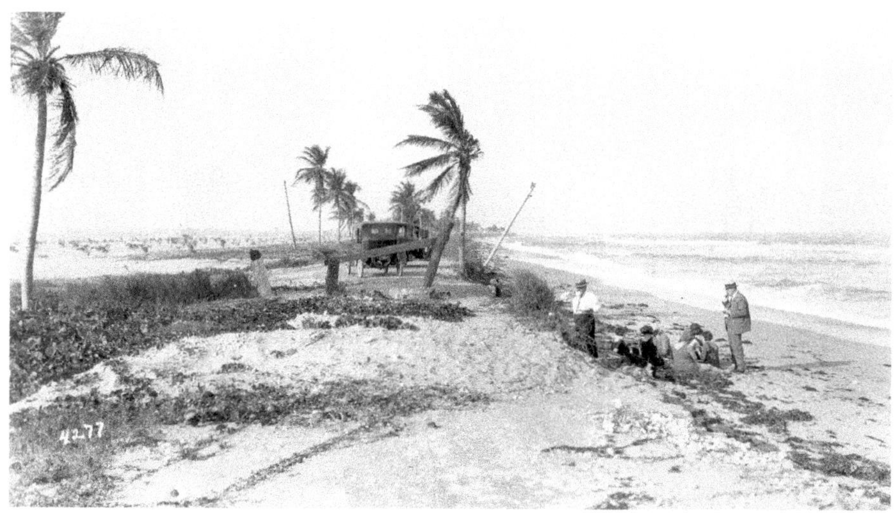

A Sunday picnic on the old Ocean Drive in 1924. *Courtesy HistoryMiami, Claude Matlack Collection 139-14.*

of the most popular of the numerous pleasure drives around the city."[59] In 1920, Thomas Pancoast reported to Carl Fisher that blacks were going "up the beach between Snowden's property and the House of Refuge and [they] park the cars along Ocean Drive and go in and bathe."[60] This was before the cut at Baker's Haulover was made; the land was still a peninsula.

In a newspaper article, E.F. Flannery described the pleasures of this Ocean Drive:

> *Swinging out of the residential section of Miami Beach northward in an automobile, there first comes over the traveler the invigorating yet soft touches of the trade winds, skipping across the blue-green waters landward, leaving in their wake a mass of silvery capped waves which seem to beckon a salutation. The automobile swerves nearer the ocean, on to the wending, narrow roadway of black where the swaying fronds of the palms above blend harmoniously with the hum of the motorcar's engine and the reassuring, incessant lapping of the breakers along the beach…Drive over the same route three hours later, just about the time the full tropical moon edges its way out of the waters to the east…The fronds of the palm trees sway as before. Strange shadows now darken the dark gray roadway ahead of the automobile. The east wind is just a bit gentler. The moon rises rapidly, flooding the ocean with its light,*

> *and romance stalks at every turn. The automobile is brought to a halt. The lights are extinguished. There is the call of the night bird, the small breakers on the beach. All else is quiet.*[61]

Within a few years, Carl Fisher's land development companies had acquired all the oceanfront land from the city limits north to Sixty-ninth Street. Fisher envisioned creating a "millionaires' row" of winter estates here. In 1920, his Miami Ocean View Company filed the First Oceanfront Subdivision, extending along the shoreline from Forty-ninth to about Fifty-sixth Street. In April 1924, his Miami Beach Bay Shore Company filed the Second Oceanfront Subdivision, extending from Fifty-sixth to Sixty-ninth Street. Both of these subdivisions lay in unincorporated Dade County at the time of their filing, outside the Miami Beach city limits

The road, however, cut off Carl Fisher's "Oceanfront Subdivisions" from the oceanfront. Wealthy investors were unwilling to build their winter homes where carloads of sightseers were driving along the shoreline. Although Fisher had made a fortune with his Prest-O-Lite company, he had borrowed against all he had to build the Flamingo Hotel and other

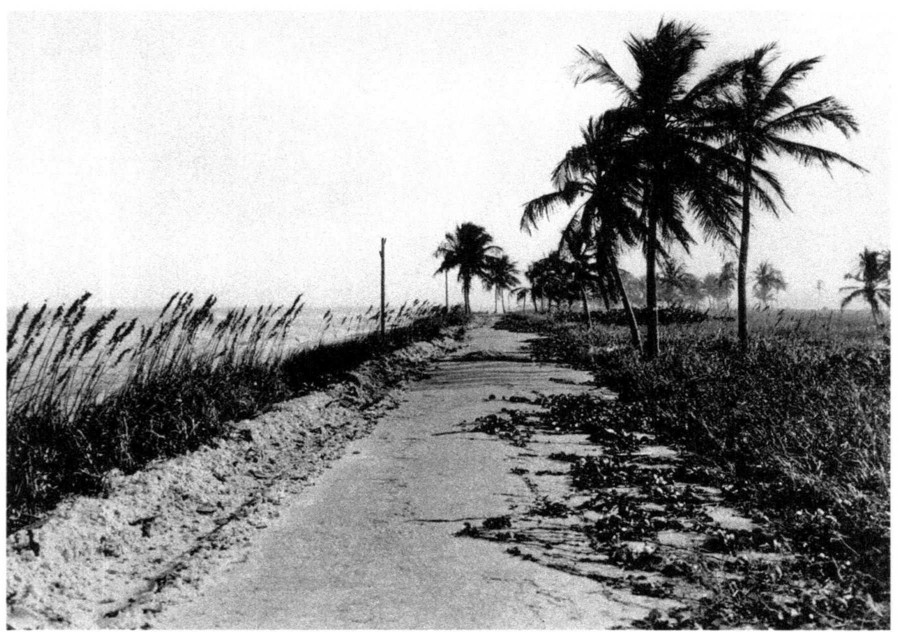

"Ocean Drive, partially destroyed" in November 1924. *Courtesy City of Miami Beach Historical Archive.*

projects, so selling this land was crucial. He built a parallel road along Indian Creek, a short distance to the west, as a more desirable alternate route and then petitioned the county to condemn Ocean Drive, arguing that it had been built privately in the first place. But public outcry kept the county from closing the scenic road.

Fisher then got the Miami Beach City Council to pass an ordinance extending the city limits, putting this stretch of the road under its jurisdiction. This ordinance was to go into effect on May 15, 1924,[62] but the public still fought to save the old roadway, and a long legal wrangle ensued. On Fisher's side, one investor, Eugene Couture, built a house directly on the roadbed at Forty-ninth Street.[63] Other parts of the road were dynamited and barricaded at night in an effort to make it unusable.[64] Fisher's manager, Walter Kohlhepp, wrote to Fisher in July:

> *In order to speed things up I asked* [Judge] *Will Price to investigate and advise as to the possibility of destroying the old road in spite of the armed guards insofar as it affected our property and he has just stated that we are perfectly within our rights...I believe that this would help bring matters to a head and speed things up if we were to take our 10-ton Holts and tear up the road for a good distance at each end. I don't doubt but that the Sheriff will arrest one or two of our men while this is being done, but there is no chance of them making a case of it.*[65]

On the other side, an injunction by the residents of Harding Townsite (between Seventy-third and Seventy-fifth Streets), who protested having to pay Miami Beach taxes, held up the boundary expansion for weeks.[66] (Ocean Terrace in that section today is a remnant of the disputed Ocean Drive.)

The city limits ordinance was eventually upheld in court, a move that increased the territory of Miami Beach by 75 percent, but it received only incidental mention in the newspapers. This is the extent of the *Miami Herald*'s coverage on July 2, 1924:

> *Contingent upon further court action to stop extension of Miami Beach city limits, the limits were considered extended yesterday three miles north of the former line, which was near the Snowden estate. The limit line now extends east and west across the territory north of the house of refuge, and includes Altos del Mar and other subdivisions. About the only noticeable change in the status of affairs was that the building inspector's office prepared to supervise any building that might be attempted in that locality, and the street*

and alley department as well as the engineering force became cognizant of additional area under their jurisdiction.[67]

Today, this long-lost Ocean Drive is not even a memory, and E.F. Flannery's prediction in 1924, which was off by only a block, has come true: "Unless public spirit prevails or legal intervention is successful, within another year, the only Ocean Drive at Miami Beach will be that between Biscayne avenue [*sic*] and Fourteenth street."[68]

THE SURFSIDE SITE

The Tatum brothers platted six Altos del Mar subdivisions in what is now the north end of Miami Beach and the adjoining town of Surfside. They platted Altos del Mar One and Two in 1919 along the ocean north of the house of refuge. Altos del Mar Three, to the west of One, followed in 1923.

Altos del Mar Four, Five and Six, platted in 1923 and 1924, extended from the ocean to Indian Creek between Ninetieth and Ninety-sixth

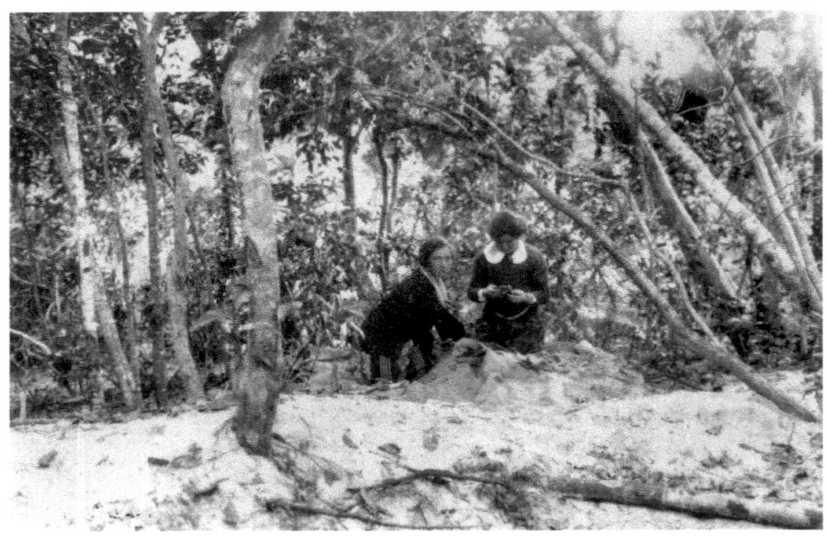

The wife of botanist John K. Small and a friend explore the prehistoric Surfside mound in the 1920s. *Courtesy Arva Moore Parks, Miami News collection.*

Streets, in what later became the town of Surfside. It was here in 1923, in the process of building Bay Drive along Indian Creek, that the Tatums unearthed a burial mound containing numerous skulls that were later determined to be those of Tequesta Indians, of uncertain date. Unfortunately, after an initial flurry of publicity, the bones were dispersed, and most of the site was paved over. Archaeologists did not excavate the site until there were two digs, in 1933–34 and in 1935. The first was directed by Florida state archaeologist Vernon Lamme[69] and the second by Karl Squires and Dr. Julian H. Steward.

The site consisted of a 372-foot-long habitation mound on Bay Drive between Ninety-first and Ninety-third Streets and a burial mound at the corner of Bay Drive and Ninety-fourth Street that measured seventy feet east-to-west and twenty feet north-to-south. The 1934 excavation found the remains of at least fifty people, including a group of nineteen skulls in the burial mound. The habitation mound contained potsherds, arrowheads, bone tools and artifacts of shell and stone.[70] All the 1934 finds were to be sent to the Smithsonian Institution in Washington, D.C., but they were stolen before shipment. Additional artifacts from the 1935 dig made it there successfully, and they are catalogued by numbers 384324 to 384525 at the Smithsonian as Glades Culture artifacts from the Surfside Site.

CHAPTER 6

MILLIONAIRES' ROW

After Carl Fisher got rid of the oceanfront road, wealthy northern men began to buy his lots along the shoreline and to build elegant winter homes with their own private beaches. When the high-class, private Bath Club opened in 1927 on the beach at Fifty-ninth Street, the mile-and-a-half stretch of oceanfront between the Snowden (Firestone) estate and the Bath Club came to be known as "Millionaires' Row." This is a narrow isthmus of land between the ocean and Indian Creek, affording privacy and seclusion a few miles north of the city center.

The Bath Club still survives, but all the mansions in this section are gone. All forty of them, some larger than others, were completed by 1939. They are listed in the table that follows, with as much information as survives in city building records and elsewhere. Before you laugh at the cost of these estates, this is roughly what *$10,000* in the following years would be worth in 2014:[71]

1920: $118,500
1925: $135,000
1930: $141,500
1935: $172,500

While some of these folks added swimming pools, none of the homes had air conditioning at first. And the cost of the houses, of course, does not include the land. Most of these are large lots, one hundred feet wide and four hundred or more feet deep from ocean to road. Some estates occupied several lots. In 1929, William Griffin paid $90,000 for a one-hundred-foot lot, and a double lot cost Albert Erskine $157,500. For a comparable figure in 2014, multiply by fourteen.

At around Fifty-fifth Street (although there are no cross streets here), Collins Avenue bends eastward and bisects this strip of land so that there are smaller lots on both sides. Even-numbered addresses are on Indian Creek, and the odd-numbered addresses are on the ocean. Lots here were two hundred feet deep and only seventy-five feet wide. As the table shows, the homes were less costly in this section.

Besides the beauty of the place, a major incentive for the wealthy to build here was a proposal by the Florida legislature in 1923, subsequently adopted in the state constitution, forever prohibiting state income or inheritance taxes:

> *This was a long step in advance for Florida to take at a time when every other State in the Union was either imposing such taxes or contemplating their imposition. It was adopted with the frankly avowed purpose of inducing persons of wealth to make Florida their legal residence.*[72]

Most of the Miami Beach millionaires, like Carl Fisher himself, had rags-to-riches stories. Many had made their fortunes in modern industries, especially automobiles and their accoutrements—oil, tires, headlights, carburetors, gas pumps. The "old money" of East Coast society who had inherited their wealth built their winter homes in Palm Beach. The Miami Beach millionaires were the *nouveaux riches*, largely from the Midwest, who had risen through hard work, vision and a bit of luck.

ARCHITECTS

Those familiar with Florida architects in this era will notice some famous names in the table. In alphabetical order, these are among the better known:

WALTER C. DEGARMO (1876–1951), "Dean of Miami architects,"[73] was born in Illinois and educated in civil engineering at Swarthmore and in architecture at Cornell. He worked first in Philadelphia and New York; when he moved to Coconut Grove in 1903, he was the first university-trained architect in South Florida. In Miami, Miami Beach and Coral Gables, he designed civic buildings, theaters, schools, churches, residences

THE MANSIONS OF MILLIONAIRES' ROW

ADDRESS	ARCHITECT	DATE	OWNER(S)	COST	DEMOL
4401 Collins	Herbert Bass	1916	Snowden, Firestone	$60K	1954
4537 "	R.T. Pancoast	1929	Griffin, Warner	$70K	1955
4545 "	Kiehnel & Elliott	1925	Elston, McCullough	$65K	1955
4621 "	Kiehnel & Elliott	1924	B.H. Sherman	$45K	1963
4747 "	C.B. Schoeppl	1939	M. Foote	$50K	1961
4813–17 "	Wyeth & Geiger	1929	A. Erskine	$185K	1963
4855 "	A. Geiger	1927	J.B. Ford	$93.3K	1962
4909 "	--- (H. Major, 1928)	1924	Couture, (Hertz)	($48.5K)	1963
4925 "	H. Major	1928	A. Lasker	$80K	1954
5005 "	W. Lingler	1930	L. Sigman	$75K	1963
5027 "	M.L. Hampton	1931	W.G. Potts	$75K	1963
5041 "	R.L. Weed	1935	E.B. Orr	$56K	1962
5151–67 "	Treanor/Fatio/Schoeppl	1934	W.O. Briggs	$108K	1965
5197 "	Beach Construction Co.	1925	F.Tod	$60K	1965
5209 "	Kiehnel & Elliott	1925	E.M. Johnson	$35K	1962
5225 "	Wyeth & Bruno	1929	W. Taradash	$127K	1962
5255 "	M.L. Hampton	1932	W. Wright	$150K	1961
5333 "	H. Major	1928	H.T. Archibald	$55K	1959
5349 "	A. Geiger	1926	Carl Fisher, W. Noll	$85K	1959
5361–69 "	DeGarmo & Varney	1925	Ferris, Schenck	$30K	1967
5377 "	DeGarmo	1928	E.H. Gold, Schenck	$175K	1967
5401 "	M.L. Hampton	1934	Green, Plimpton	$50K	1967
5445 "	Schoeppl & Southwell	1936	Mendelson	$80K	1966
5470 "	F.W. Woods	1929	McClure, Farnsworth	$40K	1967
5545 "	Contractor C.R.Clark	1928	Dr. A. Variel	$48K	1963
5555 "	Schoeppl & Southwell	1936	J. Kugelman	$25K	1963
5574 "	G.E. Mayer	1926	Gar Wood	$45K	1965
5640 "	R.A. Taylor	1937	N.B.T. Roney	$45K	1966
5641 "	F.W. Woods	1929	F. Gannett	$50K	1966
5666 "	F.W. Woods	1929	Jones, Meade	$25K	1968
5690 "	R.L. Weed	ca. 1935	L. Schwab	?	?
5706 "	R.M. Little	1934	United Services Corp.	$25K	1966
5720 "	T.H. Henderson	1936	H.M. Hardee	$25K	1966
5742 "	Hummings Constr. Co.	1925	McClure, Peterson	$20K	1967
5743–47 "	R.T. Pancoast	1937	G. A. Bell	$45K	1975
5750 "	C.B. Schoeppl	1933	United Services Corp.	$21K	1968
5780 "	J. Bullen	1935	D.J. Slenker	$25K	1967
5800 "	F.W. Woods	1928	Lindsay Hopkins	$24.5K	1967
5801 "	Schoeppl & Southwell	1937	E. Zorilla	$24K	1983
5825 "	Schoeppl & Southwell	1935	N. Boice Co.	$45K	1961
5838 "	R.T. Pancoast	1929	H.A. Clark	$35K	?

and commercial buildings, mostly in the Mediterranean style. George A. Varney from New York was his partner in several Miami Beach projects. (In 1916, Varney became known for setting a legal precedent: a dispute with his New York employer regarding promised payment resulted in a landmark court case, *Varney v. Ditmars*, that set standards for verbal agreements.)

August Geiger (1888–1968) moved to Miami from Connecticut in 1905 and became the tenth registered architect in Florida in 1915. Trained largely by apprenticeship, he worked in the Beaux-Arts style, designing many early schools in Dade County and the first Miami City Hospital. In Miami Beach, he was Carl Fisher's favored architect. Geiger designed the Lincoln Apartments, the Beaux-Arts Building, Allison Hospital, La Gorce Golf Clubhouse and two Beaux-Arts municipal water towers—all lost. Still surviving are his Golf Clubhouse on the Collins Canal, the Van Dyke Building on Lincoln Road, the Ida Fisher School on Drexel Avenue and Carl Fisher's residence on North Bay Road. Geiger also invested in real estate and was active in many local civic groups.

Martin L. Hampton (1891–1950) was from South Carolina and graduated from Columbia University in New York. He came to Miami in 1914 and returned here after serving in World War I. In 1923, he traveled through Spain for firsthand study of Mediterranean architecture, and he was acknowledged as a master of this style in Florida, in Palm Beach, Miami, Coral Gables and Miami Beach. See Chapter 10 for more on his lost works.

Kiehnel and Elliott was a Pittsburgh firm that came to Miami in 1917 to design a winter estate in Coconut Grove for steel magnate John Bindley. Richard Kiehnel (1870–1944), a native of Germany, decided to move to Miami, opened a branch office for the firm and designed some of the Miami area's most beautiful buildings. (There is no evidence that his partner, John Elliott, ever came to Florida.) What distinguishes Kiehnel's design style, whether Mediterranean or Art Deco, is a combination of overall grandeur and exquisitely fine decorative detail, particularly lacy, perforated masonry. In Miami Beach, Kiehnel & Elliott designed a few residences, commercial buildings and hotels, including the King Cole Hotel for Carl Fisher. Residences were most often in the Mediterranean style. Surviving Art Deco structures include the Nunnally Building on Lincoln Road and the Carlyle Hotel on Ocean Drive.

Howard B. Major (1882–1974) was from New York and moved to Palm Beach in 1925 to work with Addison Mizner, who specialized in the Mediterranean style. Major himself preferred the Georgian style for Florida, feeling it was a more appropriate reference to the British West Indies.[74] He designed very few buildings in Miami Beach, apparently only residences.

RUSSELL T. PANCOAST (1899–1972), the grandson of John S. Collins, was born in New Jersey, joined his family in Miami Beach in 1913 and returned here after earning a degree in architecture from Cornell in 1922. His wife, Katherine, was a classmate, and for their honeymoon, they traveled to Spain, Italy and North Africa to study Mediterranean architecture. Pancoast worked for Kiehnel & Elliott, became manager of their Miami Beach office in 1924 and started his own practice in 1928. His first "big job" was designing the prestigious Surf Club in Surfside in 1929. His other surviving work includes the Collins Memorial Library, now the Bass Museum of Art, in Miami Beach.

CARLOS B. SCHOEPPL (1898–1990) was born in Texas and studied architecture at UCLA. A larger-than-life character, he had an early interest in aviation and counted Howard Hughes and Eddie Rickenbacker among his friends, who called him "Shep." He moved to Jacksonville in 1926 to work with developer D.P. Davis and came to Miami Beach in 1933. Despite the Depression, he received many commissions to design luxurious winter homes for the wealthy along Florida's "Gold Coast,"[75] specializing in the Mediterranean style. In the 1930s, he partnered with Arnold Southwell, who was born in Washington State and had worked in New York City.

ROBERT LAW WEED (1897–1961), a native of Pennsylvania, studied architecture and engineering at the Carnegie Institute of Technology in Pittsburgh and served in both world wars. He moved to Miami in 1919 to study under Richard Kiehnel and opened a private practice in 1922.[76] Weed's style was modern, and he is credited with designing the Florida Model House for the 1933 Chicago World's Fair.[77] He was one of the primary architects of the University of Miami campus in Coral Gables. In Miami Beach, he designed the Kennel Club, the Beach Theatre (both demolished), the Twenty-third Street Fire Station and a number of residences.

FRANK WYATT WOODS (1894–1962) was a graduate of Brown University and the Rhode Island School of Design, and he came to Miami in 1924. His architectural style evolved from Vernacular to Mediterranean to Art Deco to Postwar Modern; most of his surviving buildings are in Normandy Isle and northern Miami Beach. He was an honorary member of the American Institute of Architects.[78]

MARION SIMS WYETH (1889–1982) graduated from Princeton in 1910, attended the Paris École des Beaux-Arts in 1914 and then worked for Bertram Goodhue and Carrere & Hastings in New York. Living in Palm Beach from 1919 until his death, he designed many Mediterranean-style homes there and the Florida governor's mansion in Tallahassee in 1957.[79]

THE MANSIONS AND THEIR OWNERS

After the 1916 Snowden estate, described in Chapter 3, the next house to be built along this stretch of beach was Eugene Couture's, built in 1924 directly on the roadbed in order to challenge the road's existence. It occupied the first lot in the First Oceanfront Subdivision, at 4901 Collins Avenue. Couture was probably not a millionaire; he had been a theater manager in Manchester, New Hampshire, and his beach home was a modest two-story masonry building with two small towers. In 1927, car rental and Yellow Cab founder John D. Hertz from Chicago bought it and made it more luxurious. After more than $15,000 in preliminary alterations, Hertz hired Palm Beach architect Howard Major to design a $48,500 addition to the house in 1928.

At the same time as Hertz's addition, Major was also designing an $80,000 estate on the next lot to the north, for advertising maven Albert D. Lasker. Another Chicagoan, Lasker (1880–1952) was the former chairman of the U.S. Shipping Board and, by 1928, was president of Lord, Thomas & Logan, one of the world's largest advertising agencies.[80] He is considered the father of modern advertising, employing psychological strategies and using the new mass medium of radio. Whether or not Hertz and Lasker knew each other from Chicago, they became close friends as next-door neighbors on the beach. Both were Jewish. According to Polly Redford,

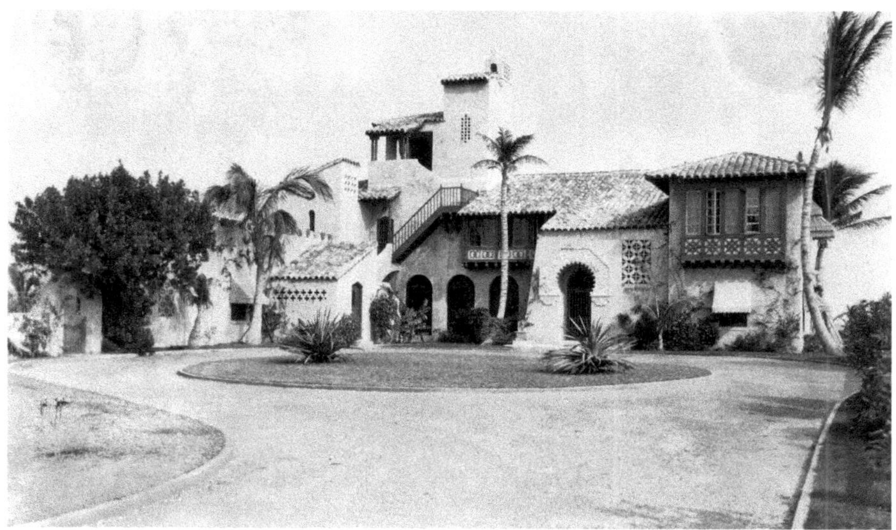

The Isaac Elston estate, designed by Kiehnel & Elliott in 1925 and later occupied by Chicago banker Charles A. McCullough. *Courtesy HistoryMiami, Claude Matlack Collection 214-2.*

"Together they made a golden ghetto so exclusive that when a third Jewish gentleman proposed to build next door they implored Fisher not to sell him the property."[81] Redford does not name the gentleman in question, but it may have been Leon Sigman, owner of the Scotch Woolen Mills in Chicago, who built the house north of Lasker in 1930.

Shortly after his house was completed, Lasker hosted U.S. vice president Charles Curtis for a six-day stay. Herbert Hoover and Curtis had won the election in November 1928. They took office on March 4, 1929 (Inauguration Day in January didn't go into effect until 1934), and Curtis arrived in Miami by train on March 10. (Hoover had just visited Miami Beach in January as president-elect.) Curtis himself was a former jockey, and his stay included a day at the Hialeah races with Lasker and the Hertzes. The following day, Carl Fisher took Curtis, Lasker and Harvey Firestone on a fishing trip to his island hideaway, Cocolobo Cay, and the following evening, Firestone hosted a reception for Curtis at his estate, attended by 150 guests.[82]

In January 1930, a colleague of John Hertz moved into a house a few lots to the south of his, at 4545 Collins Avenue. It had been built in 1925 for Isaac C. Elston Jr., a banker from Indiana who kept his yacht docked at the Nautilus Hotel. Designed by Kiehnel & Elliott, the house originally cost $65,000. The new buyer in December 1929 (right after the Crash) was Charles A. McCullough, "Chicago and New York financier and official of several transportation companies."[83] He paid $230,000 for it, but that included the land and possibly the furnishings:

> *Mr. McCullough and Mr. Hertz were executives of the Yellow Cab Company during the period when it became one of the world's leading transportation corporations and before that time were rival, yet friendly newspapermen.*[84]

McCullough started as a newsboy on Chicago's west side and rose to management at the *Chicago Tribune* and the *Evening Post*. Hertz, meanwhile, was a reporter for the *Chicago Record*. When Hertz resigned as chairman of the Yellow Cab Company, McCullough, who was vice-president, succeeded him.

McCullough's house was a sprawling Mediterranean extravaganza by Kiehnel & Elliott, with multiple barrel-tile roofs, their signature perforated masonry, a lacy keyhole arch and a projecting oriel window. The photograph on the preceding page is from 1925. Mr. McCullough put in $50,000 additions in 1930 and a $12,000 swimming pool in 1936.

Kiehnel & Elliott had also designed the next house to the north, at 4621 Collins Avenue, in 1924. It was built for B.H. Sherman and was

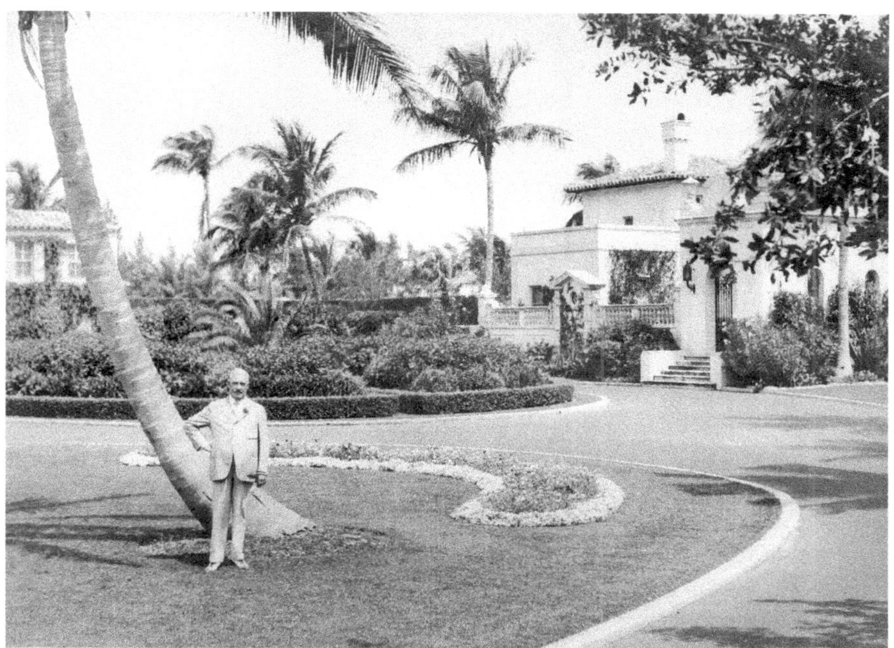

John B. Ford from Detroit at his home at 4855 Collins Avenue, designed by August Geiger in 1927. *Courtesy City of Miami Beach Historical Archive.*

later bought by J. Richard Francis of the Marvel Carburetor Company of Detroit. Another Kiehnel & Elliott home at 5902 Collins Avenue was built in 1925 for E. Meade Johnson, of the medical supply company in New Brunswick, New Jersey.

John Hertz's neighbor to the south was John B. Ford, who was president of the Michigan Alkali Corporation in Detroit.[85] His $93,300 winter home at 4855 Collins Avenue occupied three lots and was designed in 1927 by Carl Fisher's favorite architect, August Geiger, in his signature Beaux-Arts style.

Next door to the south of Ford, Albert R. Erskine bought two lots in early 1929 that cost nearly as much as the $185,000 house that Marion Wyeth and August Geiger designed for him there. Erskine was from South Bend, Indiana, and was president of the Studebaker Corporation (that also made Pierce Arrows), a director of the Federal Reserve Bank of Chicago and on the board of directors for Notre Dame University. He decided to build a winter home here after visiting the Firestones.[86]

August Geiger is represented by one other, more modest house here that he designed for Carl Fisher in 1926, shortly before the hurricane, at 5349

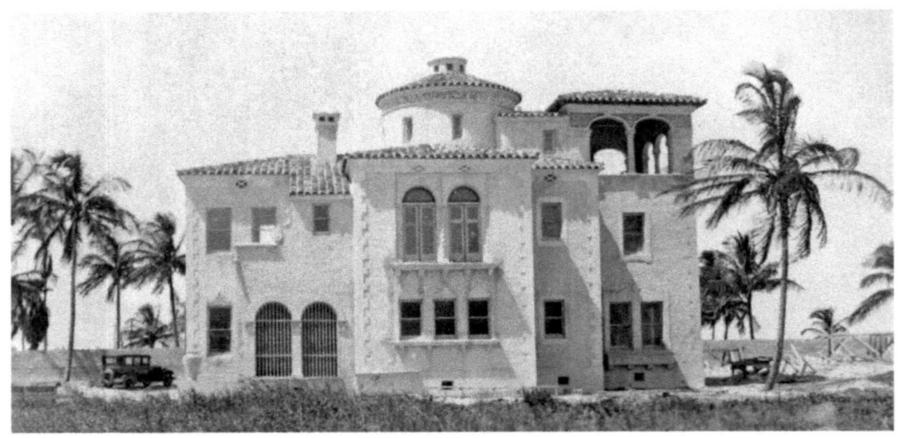

August Geiger designed this house at 5349 Collins Avenue for Carl Fisher in 1926, shortly before the hurricane. It became the home of William H. Noll from Indiana. *Courtesy City of Miami Beach Historical Archive.*

Collins Avenue. Fisher sold it to William H. Noll, a drug manufacturer from Fort Wayne, Indiana.

Just north of the Noll residence, DeGarmo & Varney had designed a house in 1925 for Warren B. Ferris of Columbus, Ohio, that was purchased by New York stockbroker Nicholas Schenck. In February 1928, a building permit was issued for another estate to be designed by DeGarmo on the two adjoining lots to the north, at 5377 Collins Avenue. This was to be the $175,000 winter home of Egbert H. Gold of Holland, Michigan. Gold was president of the Vapor Car Heating Company that made heating equipment for railroads and streetcars Gold had patented. He had stayed at Miami Beach previously and was a member of the Bath Club and the Indian Creek Golf Club, but before he could move into this new winter estate, he died at his Michigan home on November 3, 1928.[87] Based on city directory listings, it appears that Nicholas Schenck purchased the property and combined it with his neighboring home for an expansive three-lot domain. Palm Beach architects Treanor & Fatio added a $20,000 swimming pool for him in 1936.

Next to the Firestone estate at the south end of Millionaires' Row, Russell T. Pancoast designed a Mediterranean-style estate in 1929 for William M. Griffin, president of the Wayne Pump Company in Fort Wayne, Indiana, which made gas station pumps, tanks and compressors. He bought the land here for $90,000 from the estate of James Allison, who had died in August 1928. The house cost $70,000, but the complete estate was valued at $250,000

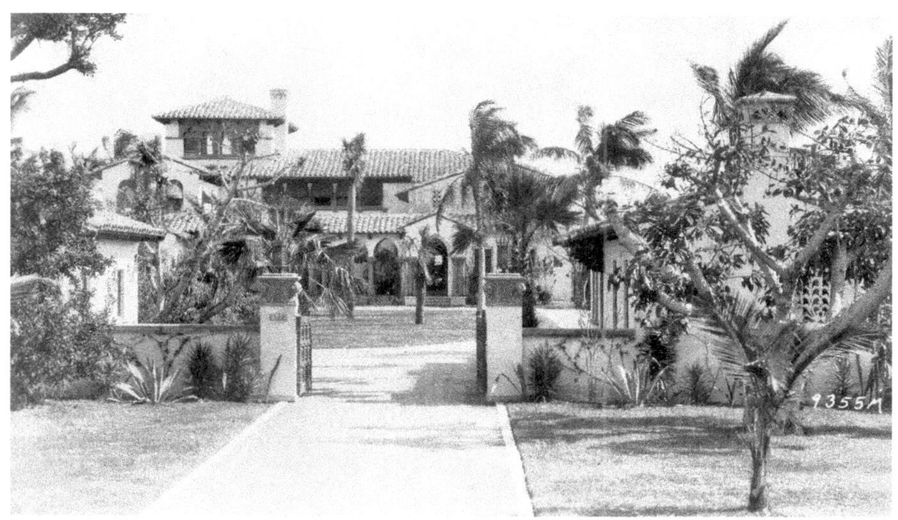

Residence of William M. Griffin, designed in 1929 by Russell T. Pancoast, later occupied by Albert Warner. *Courtesy HistoryMiami, Claude Matlack Collection 440-2.*

and was described in the newspaper: "The residence, of Sicilian architecture, will have a large patio, a large living room, and many unusual features. There will be a terrace on the ocean, a tower lounge, and six master bedrooms."[88] Albert Warner (1884–1967) owned this house for several years in the 1930s. He and his brothers, Harry, Sam and Jack, were the Warner Brothers who started a motion picture studio in 1923. Russell Pancoast added a swimming pool and other additions valued at $55,000 for him in 1937.

At the end of his life, Albert Warner had an apartment at the Imperial House at 5225 Collins Avenue. It was built in 1961 where the estate of Warren Wright had been. Wright owned Calumet Farms, of horse racing fame. Martin L. Hampton, architect of the Pancoast Hotel, designed the Wright home in 1932.

On the south side of the Wright estate was the $127,000 mansion of William Taradash, designed by Marion Sims Wyeth and Thomas A. Bruno in 1929. Taradash had been a garment maker in Chicago and president of the Sterling Manufacturing Company,[89] but he became a prominent real estate developer in Miami Beach. The Sterling Building on Lincoln Road was his, and he was one of the organizers of the Community Theatre.

Another house built here in 1929 was designed by Frank Wyatt Woods for Frank E. Gannett of Rochester, New York. Gannett owned sixteen newspapers, mostly in upstate New York. He had brought his family to Miami

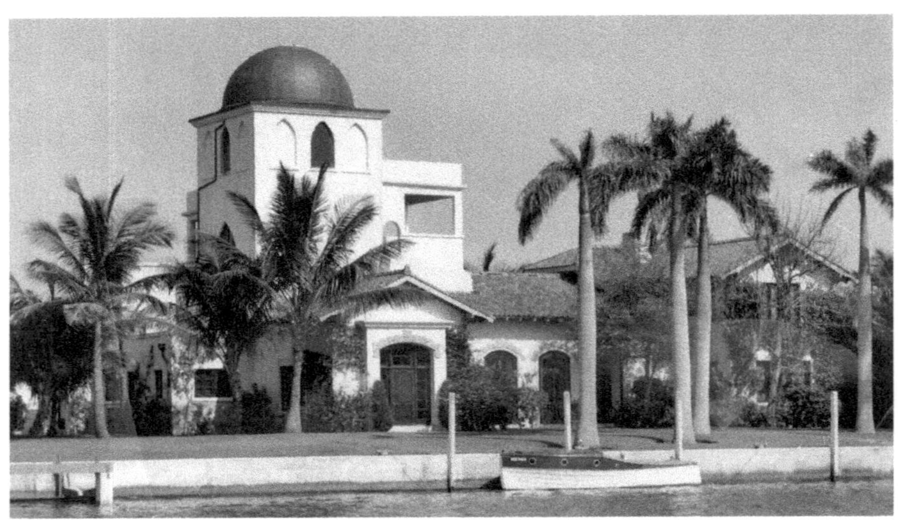

The home of speedboat racer Gar Wood, with its distinctive observatory, built in 1926. *Courtesy City of Miami Beach Historical Archive.*

Beach for the first time in early 1929 for his daughter's health, staying at the Fleetwood Hotel for three weeks and then moving to the Lincoln. After only three days, he decided to buy one of the smaller oceanfront lots near the Bath Club and build a winter home in time for the following season.[90]

Across Collins Avenue from Gannett's home, on one of the small lots facing Indian Creek, was the home of inventor and champion speedboat racer Gar Wood from Detroit, who was a close friend of Carl Fisher. He had invented a hydraulic lift in 1912 and "made his first million in a year."[91] The house was built in 1926, designed by Miami architect Gordon E. Mayer. Gar Wood was an amateur astronomer, and the house became a landmark for its observatory dome. Deep pilings and heavy concrete foundations to stabilize the telescope also protected the house during the hurricane that struck shortly after its completion.[92]

To the north of Gar Wood's home, also on the creek side, Robert A. Taylor designed a house for Miami Beach developer Newton B.T. Roney in 1937. Taylor designed most of Roney's buildings, including the Haddon Hotel at Fifth Street and the Spanish Village on Espanola Way. This house was in the name of Roney's wife, Gertrude, but the 1940 U.S. census shows the whole family living here, along with a "Negro" butler and maid.

No building records remain for the house at 5690 Collins Avenue, but a realty prospectus[93] identifies the architect as Robert Law Weed and the style of the three-bedroom house as Monterey, built about 1935. The Monterey style for homes, popular from the 1920s to 1950s, originated much earlier in California as a combination of New England colonial and Spanish adobe construction. Usually, these homes were of two stories, with covered porches on both floors and sloped, shingled roofs, as opposed to clay tile.[94] This house, on the creek side, was the home of writer, columnist and theatrical producer Laurence Schwab (1890–1951), who co-produced several Broadway plays with Rodgers and Hammerstein.[95]

Another of the homes by Martin L. Hampton was built in 1931 for William G. Potts of Chicago, at 5027 Collins Avenue, and included a swimming pool. A society periodical described it as "Moorish-Spanish style," with "cloistered patios [and] latticed verandas," yet it was "charming in its simplicity."[96]

Of the seven homes designed here in the 1930s by Carlos B. Schoeppl, probably the most magnificent was the Walter O. Briggs estate on two lots at 5151–67 Collins Avenue. This $110,000 residence with elevator, garage and swimming pool was designed in the depths of the Depression in 1934 by Schoeppl together with the renowned firm of William Treanor and Maurice Fatio of New York and Palm Beach.

Walter Briggs (1877–1952) had started out in the yards of the Michigan Central Railroad upholstering railroad cars and then worked for a carriage builder and, later, the body shop for Ford and Olds automobiles. He bought out other firms to create the Briggs Manufacturing Company, dealing in auto upholstery and convertible tops and stamping sheet metal for auto bodies.

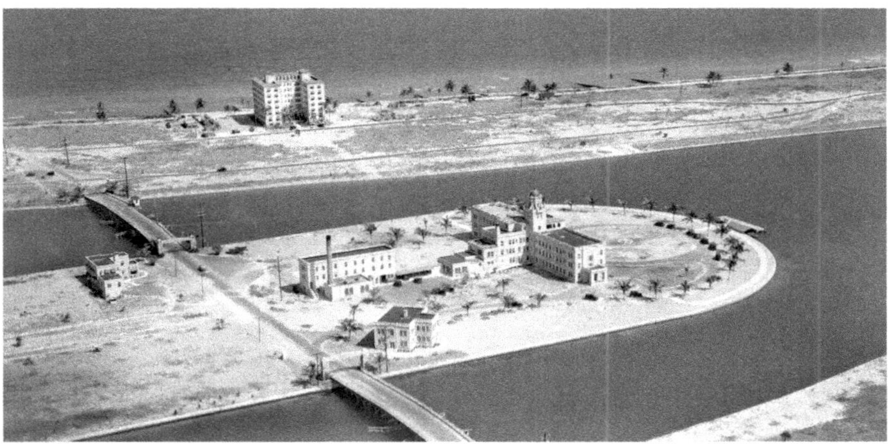

At the south end of Allison Island in Indian Creek, August Geiger designed the Allison Hospital in 1925. On the oceanfront nearby are the Gulfstream Apartments in this March 1926 view. *Courtesy of HistoryMiami, MBVCA Collection; Richard B. Hoit, photographer.*

By 1924, he was a multimillionaire and one of the country's largest suppliers of auto bodies for Ford, Chrysler, Packard and Hudson. In 1920, he became part owner—and in 1935, sole owner—of the Detroit Tigers baseball team. The ballpark in Detroit was named Briggs Field in 1938 (renamed Tigers Stadium in 1961).[97]

Just beyond Millionaires' Row, in Indian Creek at Sixtieth Street, Carl Fisher had created an island and named it for his Prest-O-Lite partner, James Allison. After Allison sold his aquarium at Fifth Street, he built a hospital at the south end of Allison Island. August Geiger was the architect of the elegant, Beaux-Arts building, with its domed tower and fountain plaza, which opened on the first day of 1926. Hospitals—and medical care in general—were of course quite different in those times. Many people came to Florida "for their health" and to recuperate from chronic conditions in the sunshine and sea air. Allison Hospital catered especially to wealthy invalids; it was known for its gourmet cuisine, and patients stayed for long periods. As the photograph shows, its location was quite isolated. This was touted as an advantage for the patients, and it also kept the hospital from marring the carefree atmosphere that Fisher was trying to create in Miami Beach (he didn't permit any cemeteries here either). The six-story Gulfstream Apartments on the beach adjacent to the hospital were designed by Hampton & Ehmann and also opened in 1926. The Gulfstream was open from December 1 to May 31 and served as a convenient place for hospital patients' families to stay. The building had two- and three-bedroom apartments with kitchens and also quarters for guests' servants. It was torn down in 1969.

Allison Hospital didn't do well financially, and the Sisters of Saint Francis took over its management in 1927, renaming it Saint Francis Hospital. Carl Fisher died there in 1939 from complications of alcoholism. In later years, the hospital was affiliated with the Miami Heart Institute, but it was eventually demolished. Its last remnants were removed in 2001, and the Aqua residential project was built on the site.

The End of Millionaires' Row

The mansions of Millionaires' Row fell to rezoning, which the property owners themselves urged in the 1950s.

The postwar years brought Miami Beach its second boom, as well as many social shifts and the rise of the middle class. As the older generation passed

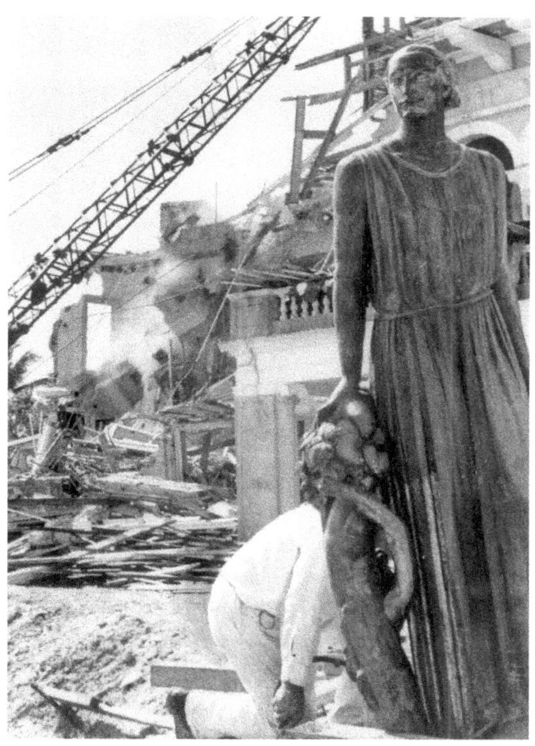

As the Firestone estate is demolished in 1954, a bronze statue of *La Normandie*, from the ship of the same name, is brought in to decorate the gardens of the new Fontainebleau Hotel. Architect Morris Lapidus had bought it as scrap metal. It returned to sea aboard the *Celebrity Summit* in 2001. *Courtesy Arva Moore Parks.*

away, families were no longer willing or able to maintain huge properties with staffs of servants. In addition, by 1949, new hotel and apartment construction had reached the property line of the Firestone estate, which was then held by the First Trust Company for Firestone's heirs. The company sued the city council to change the zoning, solely for its own lot, from the estate category enacted in 1930 (to codify what was already here) to permission for hotel use. It argued that the new neighboring hotels infringed on the estate's privacy and lowered its value; also, its property value as a hotel site would be quadruple that of a private home. The lawsuit, *City of Miami Beach v. First Trust Company*, went to the Florida Supreme Court, which ruled on March 10, 1950, that the estate zoning was unfair. The court itself did not rezone the lots; that was up to the city council.

What followed on the Firestone site, of course, was the Fontainebleau Hotel in 1954, but even before that, the legal precedent had started the dominoes falling. By 1952, Sam Kay, "Beach financier,"[98] who owned the property immediately north of Firestone's, started a similar lawsuit. The Florida Supreme Court made the same ruling for Kay in December 1953.

As a result, the Griffin/Warner and Elston/McCullough estates were torn down, and the Eden Roc Hotel replaced them.

There were arguments on both sides. The city council was reluctant to rezone such a large area all at once, fearing that rapid new construction would be of poor quality and would also compete with established hotels. The council created two "buffer zones" of city land to mitigate the effects of rezoning: one was a vacant stretch north of the Warren Wright estate, and the other was just north of the Eden Roc. The Sherman/Francis home by Kiehnel & Elliott stood on the latter site, where it remained as a public comfort station and lifeguard office until it was demolished in 1963.

Not all these lots went directly from estates to the condo buildings we see there today. Two hotels, now lost, were built here in the intervening years. The Royal York Hotel, a small Postwar Modern–style building designed by Albert Anis, was built immediately south of the Bath Club in 1950. It was demolished in 1999 and replaced by a condominium. In 1958, the $2.1 million Montmartre Hotel was built on three vacant lots immediately south of the Erskine estate (which was still there). Four stories tall and with three hundred rooms, the Montmartre was an impressive Postwar Modern design by Melvin Grossman, who was Albert Anis's nephew.[99] But land values here demanded higher density. The Montmartre was demolished in January 1982, and the Blue and Green Diamond condo towers now stand on the site.

Millionaires' Row is of particular interest because it was a concentration of the finest homes of the era, designed by the best-known architects, built in a little more than twenty years and almost totally obliterated in even less time than that. There were, however, other outstanding homes and interesting people elsewhere in Miami Beach in the 1920s that have disappeared, too.

Chapter 7
Other Homes

Many fine old Miami Beach homes still remain, particularly on Pine Tree and La Gorce Drives, North Bay Road and the man-made islands in the bay, but of course, many hundreds have been demolished over the years. These are just a few that had especially interesting stories, plus some club buildings that give a view of social life here in times past.

William F. Whitman House

The story of the Whitman house is compelling not only because William Whitman played a major role in Miami Beach development, but also because his son Stanley has shared firsthand recollections of those times.[100]

William Francis Whitman (1859–1936) was a self-made man from Chicago who, after a year at the University of Michigan, learned the printing trade and established the Excelsior Printing Company. Started without capital, it evolved into the Whitman Publishing Company, one of the largest printing and engraving plants in Chicago. Whitman also devised a new system of operations that served as a model for other printing plants.[101]

William and his wife, Leona, had three sons: William Jr., Stanley and Dudley. About 1918, the year Stanley was born, Whitman built a home in Miami Beach, on the oceanfront just south of Thirty-third Street, where the family would come every winter in their seven-passenger Packard. "My father had to have the biggest, most expensive car made," Stanley recalls. "Every year as winter came, we'd get in the car and drive down to Florida. Before summer set in, we'd drive back to Chicago. We did it in a couple of days." Mr. Whitman drove—"and he drove fast"—with his wife and three sons, and two servants who sat in the foldout seats. "The car had a huge trunk and well fenders in front; a suitcase would fit in each one."

At that time, "the South had not recovered from the Civil War. Hotels were indescribably bad, and the roads—good God, it was red clay. When it rained, you were knee-deep in mud, and when it didn't rain, the dust came up like a snowstorm. Farmers with their mules would be in the road—It was a thrill a minute!...When you got to Florida, from Jacksonville to Saint Augustine it was brick-paved, but south of that it was sand."

When they got to Miami Beach, "it was the most godforsaken, barren sand bar. The beach was very narrow, and all the rest of it was a mangrove swamp." Still, Stanley remembers a wonderful boyhood here. "It was so unlike what it is today. Living on the ocean, my brothers and myself were totally water-related: swimming, snorkeling, water-skiing, sailboating. Our father was a gymnast. He was sixty when I was born." Still, the boys were here for the school year. Stanley graduated from Ida Fisher High School in 1939 (it became Miami Beach High in 1940), and Dudley, a year behind him, went to school with Al Capone's son, Sonny.

William Whitman, in the meantime, bought a great deal of property here. In 1922, he started a residential subdivision, Espanola Villas, on Espanola Way, and built a half dozen houses on the block between Collins and Washington Avenues. In 1925, Newton Roney bought this project from Whitman and extended it west of Washington Avenue, creating the "Spanish Village" of shops, hotels and apartments. Most of the Whitman houses were demolished in 1940, but one was moved to the Palm View neighborhood, where it still stands.

Whitman also invested in commercial property, including a number of storefronts on Lincoln Road, and in December 1922, he was president of a group of prominent residents who organized the construction of the Miami Beach Community Theatre there.

The Whitmans were still in Chicago when the great hurricane hit Miami Beach in September 1926. When they came to the house later, they found that sand had filled the ground floor, and a fishing schooner had crashed through the dining room window. The house immediately north of theirs had blown out into the ocean and stuck there. The Whitmans recovered and, in 1928, added a tea garden and outdoor dance floor to their home.

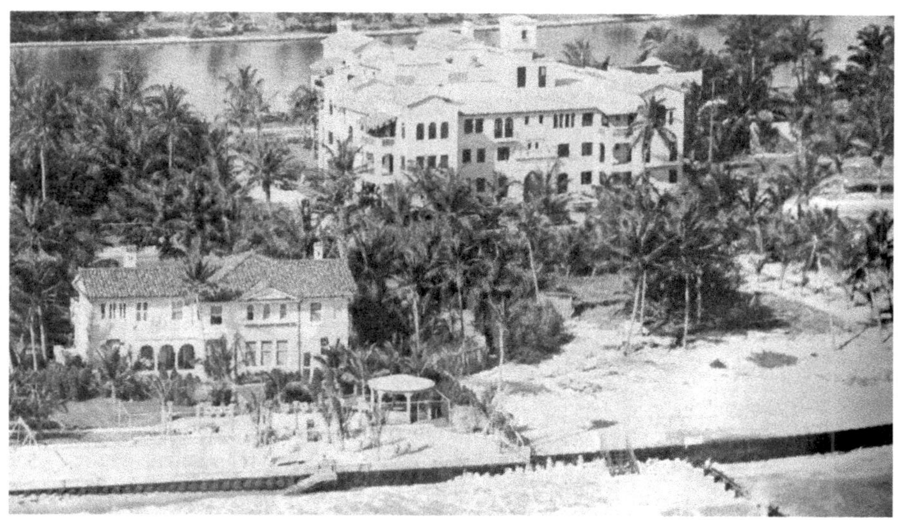

The oceanfront home of Chicago publisher William F. Whitman at left; behind it, the Indian Creek Apartments, designed by Roy F. France, are near completion in 1932. *Claude Matlack photograph in* Along Greater Miami's Sun-Sea-Ara, *courtesy Arva Moore Parks.*

One of the many good things Whitman did for Miami Beach was to bring architect Roy F. France here from Chicago in about 1930. The first of several buildings that France designed for Whitman was the Indian Creek Apartments, seen in the photograph just west of the Whitman home. In 1935, France would design the imposing Whitman Hotel on the ocean across from these apartments. The ten-story Whitman was a masterpiece of Art Deco and cost a quarter-million dollars (this during the Depression). Roy France spent the rest of his career here and designed many other landmark Miami Beach hotels. There is more on his work in Chapter 10.

William Whitman died at his beachfront home just a year later. His wife, Leona, held onto the house while still raising their sons, but after they had served in World War II and were grown and married, she sold the house to Chicago banker George D. Sax. In 1948, he demolished it and built the Saxony Hotel in its place, designed by Roy F. France. The lot to the south was sold to Ben Novack, who built the Sans Souci Hotel there in 1949, with its exterior designed by Roy France. Happily, the Saxony and Sans Souci are still standing. The profits from Mrs. Whitman's property sales went to buy land north of Miami Beach that Stanley Whitman, his son Randy and grandson Matthew went on to develop as the Bal Harbour Shops.

E.R. THOMAS HOUSE

Just up the beach from the Whitman house and built about the same time was the home of Edwin Ross Thomas, another automotive pioneer and one of the first residents here. Thomas (1850–1936) had once been "the youngest chief clerk and later, the youngest captain on the steamboats of the Mississippi and Ohio rivers."[102] He started in business with motorized bicycles and in 1900 founded the E.R. Thomas Motor Company of Buffalo, New York, manufacturing automobiles. He sold the company in 1911, and after several more transactions and mergers, it was one of many firms that eventually composed the Chrysler Corporation. Mr. Thomas, though, was most famous for building the Thomas Flyer. A 1907 model of this four-cylinder, sixty-horsepower vehicle won the around-the-world automobile race in 1908, and since this race has never been repeated, the Flyer still holds the record at 169 days.

The race, sponsored by the *New York Times*, began in Times Square on February 12, with six cars representing four nations. They reached San Francisco in a little over forty-one days, the first automotive crossing of the country. The plan was to go on by ship to Alaska, but weather conditions changed the route to Japan, then across Russia to Berlin and the finish line in Paris. The German car was first to arrive on July 26 but was disqualified for taking shortcuts. The American Flyer arrived four days later and was declared the winner; Italy came in third, and the three French entries didn't finish. Road conditions alone made this quite a feat, but the Flyer covered 13,341 miles under its own power in eighty-eight days of running time. A ship took it back to New York, where it was feted with a parade, and it is now on display at the Auto Museum in Reno, Nevada.[103]

Thomas retired from business in 1914 and came to Miami Beach. By 1920, he had built a small wood-frame house on two lots by the ocean on the north side of Fortieth Street. No original records survive, and the architect is unknown, but the house shows up in the Sanborn Fire Insurance map of January 1921. Thomas called his home Sea Weed and added to it over the years. It didn't fare well in the September 1926 hurricane:

> *We pass the home of William F. Whitman, Chicago publisher. The house fought the storm with some success but the sea wall and the heavy masonry of the front yard are gone. Next we come to a heap of ruins, the home of E.R. Thomas. Not a foot of the quaint white frame residence is standing.*[104]

A month later, undaunted and still loving the ocean, Thomas built a new two-story residence here. A 1932 periodical described the "Sea Room" at this home: separate from the main house, it was a rustic structure with an ocean view and a marine décor, including a ship's wheel and other parts, rope moldings, fishnet, wrought-iron pelicans and seashells. The ceiling had exposed beams, and the walls were paneled in pecky cypress stained sea-foam blue. Outside, there was a compass rose in the terrazzo and a rock grotto with a goldfish pond.[105]

The elderly Mr. Thomas was a beloved figure in Miami Beach who wrote poetry and threw a community Christmas party at the Roney Plaza Hotel every year. Sadly, building records document that Mr. Thomas's wonderful home was "destroyed by hurricane, 1935."[106]

JAMES M. COX HOUSE

Ohio governor James M. Cox ran for president in 1920, with Franklin Roosevelt as his running mate. (Roosevelt would contract polio the following summer.) When Warren Harding was elected instead, Cox came to Miami Beach to visit his friend Carl Fisher and decided to make a new life here. A longtime newspaperman, Cox bought the *Miami Daily Metropolis* in April

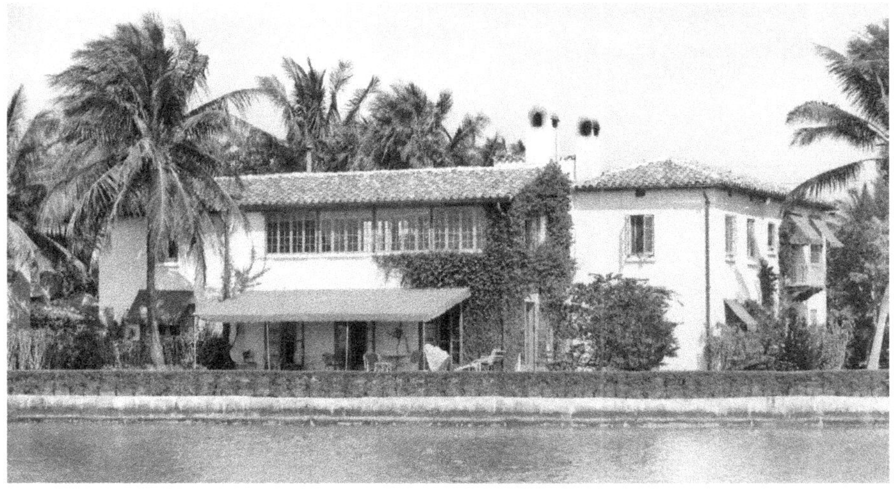

The bayside home of presidential candidate James M. Cox on North Bay Road. *Courtesy City of Miami Beach Historical Archive.*

1923 and added *News* to its name to conform with his other papers in Ohio. Eventually, it was just the *Miami News*, and Cox ran it for years.

In July 1923, he received a building permit for a $45,000 home on two lots on the bay at Forty-fourth Street, just north of where Fisher was building the Nautilus Hotel. It was a rather modest two-story Mediterranean-style house built around a central courtyard, designed by architect PHINEAS PAIST (1875–1937). Paist studied at the Pennsylvania Academy of Fine Arts and toured Europe on a scholarship in 1902. Paul Chalfin brought him to Miami to work on the James Deering estate, Villa Vizcaya, around 1915. A master of the Mediterranean style, in the 1920s, Paist went on to become supervising architect of the City of Coral Gables and a consulting architect for the new University of Miami. The Miami Beach house he designed for James Cox was demolished in 2004.

J.C. PENNEY HOUSE

James Cash Penney (1875–1971) was another well-known Miami Beach resident. Rising from an impoverished childhood in Missouri, he founded the chain of stores that still bear his name and, in January 1929, entertained President-elect Herbert Hoover in his three-story mansion on Belle Isle. It occupied Lot 8, in the southwest part of this small, circular island where all the homes were on the waterfront. Penney, however, did not build the house in the first place.

After Carl Fisher built up Belle Isle and put it on the market, the first two floors of this house were built in 1915.[107] No building records remain for this early structure, but the 1921 Sanborn map shows it as a two-story dwelling of reinforced concrete, the residence of Commodore Robert Henkle [*sic*]. The *Miami Metropolis* reported in 1916:

> *Three other palatial homes are being built on the island. The more pretentious of these is that for Commodore Robt. Henkel* [sic] *of Detroit, the cost being estimated at $30,000. In this home will be installed a $22,000 pipe organ, one of the largest in the south.*[108]

Building records do exist for the addition of the third story, documenting that it was designed for J.C. Penney in 1922 by Walter DeGarmo. Possibly, he had been the architect of the first two stories as well. The three stories

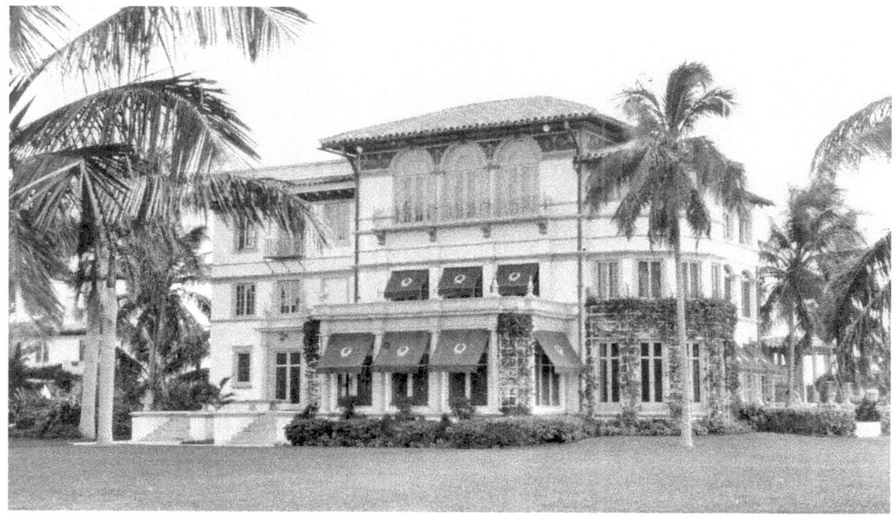

The estate of J.C. Penney on Belle Isle. Herbert Hoover was a guest here in 1929. *Postcard courtesy of Larry Wiggins.*

blended harmoniously, and the style was Italian Renaissance, with elaborate moldings, Doric pilasters, bronze-railed balconies on stone brackets and a trio of round-arched French doors at the third story. The building's shape was irregular, with a convex three-story bay on one side. The third story, which was built of hollow tile, was decorated around the roofline with a two-color frieze in sgraffito technique, and the clay tile roof "simulates as nearly as possible the roofs used in Italy."[109] The interior was described in 1925:

> *The terrace leads to the entrance door, which opens into a reception room…finished and furnished in mahogany. To the right is a superb music room. This room is one of the most notable features of the house. It is two stories high and its arched white ceiling forms a pleasing contrast with the mahogany panelings* [sic] *and furnishings of the room. In it is a three-manual organ and a grand piano, a huge period fire place, and furnishings suggestive at once of ease and elegance.*

At one end of the music room was an enclosed porch, and the dining room at the other end had a similar porch. Kitchen and servants' quarters completed the first floor. The second story was devoted to bedrooms, with a screened porch to provide a breeze without mosquitoes:

Passing on to the third story, which was added by Mr. Penney for the purpose of providing increased entertaining facilities, we come to a beautifully proportioned ball room with an octagonal loggia extension at one end and a musicians' alcove at the other end. The interior of the ball room is decorated in the style of the XVIth Century Italian work, the ceiling showing the open wood construction, elaborately painted...The remainder of the third floor is given up to guest rooms.[110]

In 1923, when his "increased entertainment facilities" were completed, Penney hosted a concert by pianist Arthur Rubenstein and violinist Paul Kochanski for 250 guests. It cost $10,000 to tear down this magnificent house in 1974. One of the many apartment towers on Belle Isle went up in its place.

DR. JOSEPH H. ADAMS HOUSE

Just east of the Penney house on Belle Isle was another impressive mansion, this one owned by Dr. Joseph H. Adams (1867–1941). Born in Brooklyn, New York, and raised in New Jersey, Adams went to medical school for a few years but "discontinued his studies in 1889...Early in 1897, Dr. Adams began experiments to make larger volumes of gasoline from crude oil possible by applying continuous heat and pressure."[111] (Called "cracking," this is not to be confused with fracking, the controversial process of extracting crude oil from the earth.) He obtained patents in 1919, worked with several oil companies and made millions. But Adams "was better known for his activities in heliotherapy research. His study of sun rays carried him to distant parts of the globe. India and the Sahara Desert were once his laboratories."[112] Adams also came to Miami and, in 1924, bought the estate of Commodore C.W. Kotcher on Belle Isle. This was a small, two-story house, plus boathouse, that Edward A. Nolan, an architect from Tennessee, had designed[113] prior to 1918.

Beside the house, Adams also bought four adjacent vacant lots from Carl Fisher Properties and planned $50,000 worth of additions and improvements, including landscaping, "an artistic teahouse" and "an elaborate boathouse, as well as replacing the existing dining room with a large dancing terrace."[114] Adams planned another $100,000 in additions in 1927. These were to include

> *a laboratory and studio building on the estate at which he will carry on his experimenting with petroleum and where he will attack, working alone as he always does, the problem of finding a prevention for tuberculosis and cure of cancer.*[115]

A later publication about the estate[116] includes many photographs and descriptions. The exterior walls were buff-colored trimmed in moss green, and the roof was dark green glazed tile. On the extensive grounds were an "Egyptian tea house" with papyrus ponds, an outdoor marble dance floor, lighted fountains and a sixty-foot dock. Inside was a mammoth studio, music room and library that had a combined piano and pipe organ. The dining room, decorated in rust and green, overlooked the bay and could seat fifty people. The second floor, with two wings, had six bedrooms. Charles Lindbergh was an overnight guest here after his first nonstop flight from New York to Miami, mapping routes to Panama. On the third floor was the master bedroom, with skylights, display space for art and a tower office cubicle that got lots of sun. In a separate structure on the waterfront Adams established his Sun Ray & Health Spa, promoting the health benefits of sunlight and saltwater baths for an assortment of ills.[117] It was managed by his son Ray[118] (and perhaps a pun was intended).

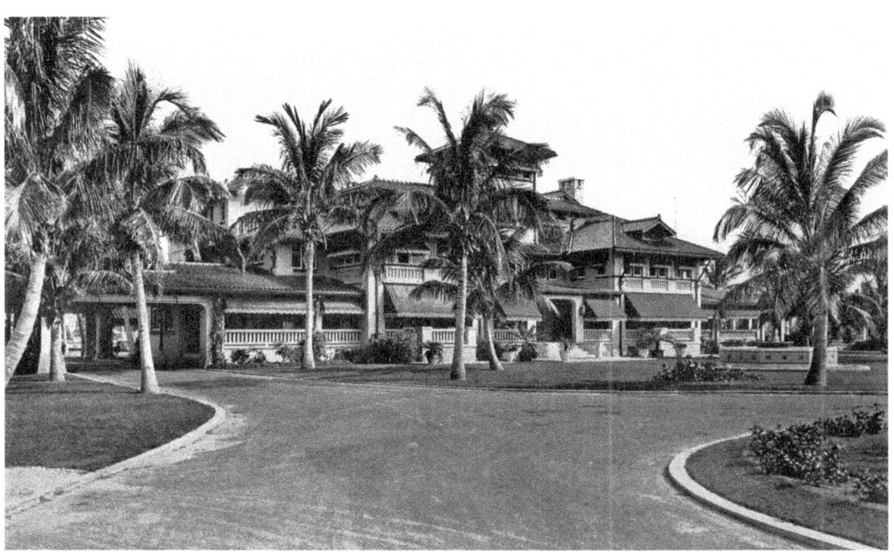

The estate of Dr. Joseph H. Adams on the southeastern shore of Belle Isle. *Courtesy City of Miami Beach Historical Archive.*

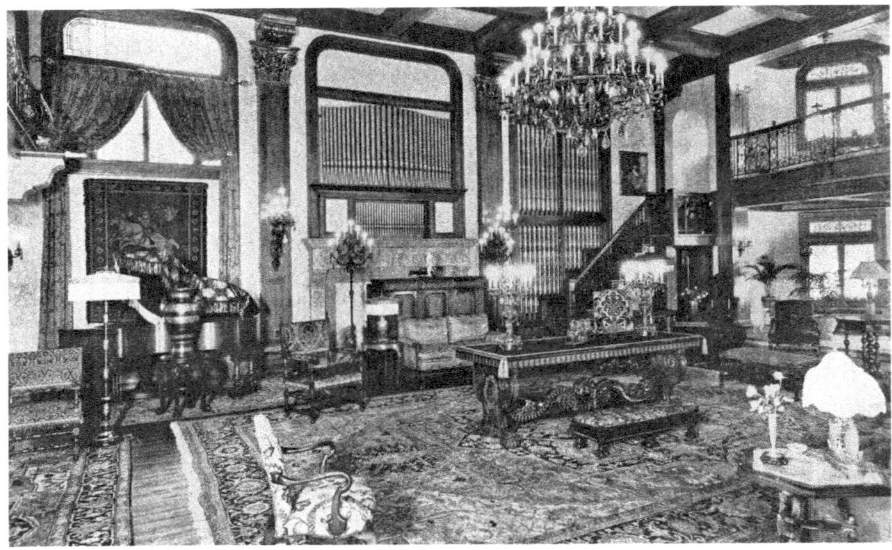

The music room in the J.H. Adams mansion had a mechanical piano and organ and could seat hundreds. It was used for church services in the 1940s. *Courtesy City of Miami Beach Historical Archive.*

Adams was also a philanthropist. Among other things, he donated $50,000 to the engineering department of the new University of Miami, which gave him an honorary doctor of science degree in 1928. In his will, he gave the boathouse of his Belle Isle estate for the University's Rosenstiel School of Marine and Atmospheric Sciences to use as a laboratory.

After Adams died in 1941, his vacant estate was leased by the newly formed congregation of All Souls, the first Episcopal church on Miami Beach. Unable to build a church because of the war, the congregation found the mansion's music room, which seated three hundred and had a built-in organ, ideal for its purposes.[119] During the war, many local residents, as well as the military trainees who were here, went to church services just to see inside the fabulous Adams estate.

In 1951, All Souls moved into its new building on Pine Tree Drive and the Adams estate next became the clubhouse for the Committee of One Hundred. This was a group of the foremost men of the city that James Allison organized in 1926, at first to clean up politics and combat gambling operations. It took on other civic, cultural and philanthropic causes; grew to three hundred members; and incorporated in 1930. World-traveled author Clayton Sedgwick Cooper was the committee's longtime president, and many of the denizens of Millionaires' Row were members. In 1951, they lost their previous meeting place near Lincoln Road and were happy to acquire the Adams estate, "establishing a clubhouse commensurate with the civic importance of the group."[120]

J.W. Popham House

As boating channels were dredged from the shallows of Biscayne Bay, islands were created from the pumped-up bay bottom. The fifty-five-acre Star Island was fashioned in this way in 1917, then given five years to dry out and settle (and for odors to dissipate) before going on the market. Besides, there was no overland way to reach it until the causeway opened in 1920. Star Island had forty-six building lots, averaging one hundred by four hundred feet, and homes built here had to cost at least $30,000.[121]

Some of the grand old Star Island mansions still survive, but one that did not was the home built in 1925 for James W. Popham (1861–1951). A native of Kentucky with an eighth-grade education, Popham made his fortune as an insurance broker throughout the South and moved his family to Atlanta in 1922. Soon after that, Popham bought a winter home on Palm Island

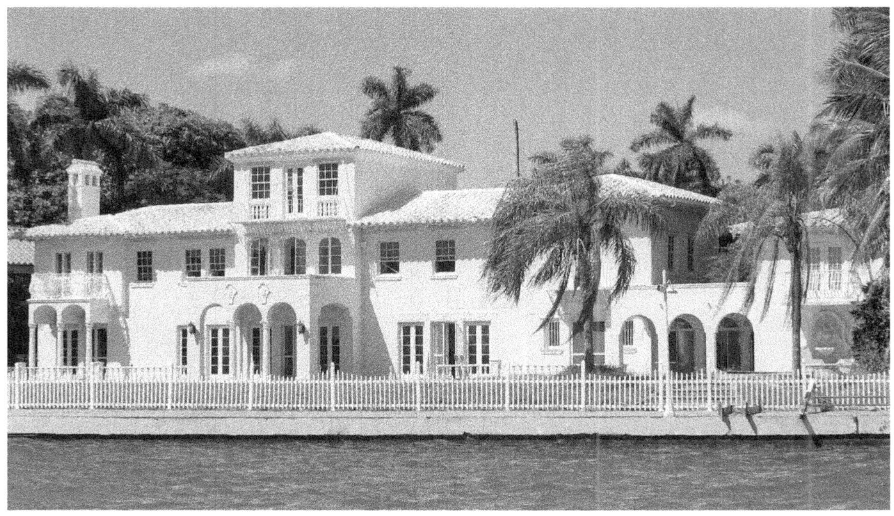

Star Island mansion designed by Walter DeGarmo for James W. Popham in 1925. It was demolished in 2014 amid much controversy. *Courtesy of Arthur Marcus, photographer.*

from realtor Clarence Busch, who lived across the street. The Pophams moved into their new, larger Star Island home in 1926. Two years later, Popham received some notoriety for selling his Palm Island property to Chicago gangster Al Capone, although this was done unknowingly through intermediaries. Popham tried unsuccessfully to void the sale.

The Popham home on Star Island was another Mediterranean confection by Walter DeGarmo and George Varney. It was a thirteen-room residence of two stories, with a three-story center section, costing $35,000. Its exterior features included barrel tile roofs, rounded arches, Corinthian columns, decorative medallions and urns and balustrades of stone and wrought iron.[122]

The owner in 2012 submitted a proposal to demolish the house and build a new one in its place that went to a public board meeting in December. Two weeks later, local preservationists formally requested that the city designate the house as a historic site to prevent its demolition. The law in some municipalities allows historic designation of private property even without the owner's consent, but such is not the case in Miami Beach. Amid much controversy, the house was demolished in 2014, which was within the owner's rights.

As we have seen, many equally fine homes in Miami Beach have been torn down over the years. What made this one a *cause célèbre* was its conspicuous location, at the south end of Star Island facing the Macarthur Causeway. Its graceful white façade was such a familiar landmark that its demolition was like losing an old friend. The issue, though, started an important dialogue and raised the question of whether private property rights are absolute or if architecture is part of the shared environment and the public should have some say in it. This is an unresolved dilemma that is by no means unique to Miami Beach.

Clarence M. Busch House

As the County Causeway was under construction, the Biscayne Bay Islands Company purchased the submerged land on the north side of the causeway and pumped up two long, parallel islands. Filling the sixty-five-acre Palm Island began in June 1919 and was completed on June 30, 1921; neighboring Hibiscus Island, with fifty-five acres, was started in 1921 and completed on April 1, 1924.[123]

Realtor Clarence Busch took out a building permit in August 1925 to construct his own $75,000 residence on the south shore of Palm Island. Its architects were George Pfeiffer, who had designed Carl Fisher's oceanfront home, and his associate Gerald J. O'Reilly, who was educated at the Massachusetts Institute of Technology.[124]

One of the most widely circulated falsehoods in Miami Beach is that Clarence Busch was heir to the famous St. Louis brewery. Eberhard Anheuser purchased this brewery in 1860. The following year, his daughter married Adolphus Busch, who had emigrated from Germany in 1857. Adolphus Busch became president of the brewery in 1880 upon the death of his father-in-law and was succeeded by his son August Busch in 1913.[125]

Clarence Marshall Busch, on the other hand, was born in Philadelphia in 1860, the son of bookbinder Joseph Busch, who was also from Pennsylvania.[126] In the 1880 U.S. census, Clarence is listed as a bookbinder, living with his mother in Philadelphia. In the 1910 census, his occupation was "real estate," and he was living with his wife and daughter in Great Neck, Long Island, New York. The family moved to Miami in 1915,[127] and in the 1920 census, Clarence, a "real estate dealer," and his family were living on Brickell Avenue in Miami. The 1930 census lists the family at 94 Palm Avenue on Palm Island, with C.M. Bush [*sic*] a "real estate broker." Busch's obituary in 1943 describes him as a "retired realtor" and "a developer of Palm Island and Hibiscus Island," "a philanthropist" and "author of several religious works."[128] Nowhere has any association with the brewery been found.

The Busch home on Palm Island became "a famous gathering place for literary people and artists."[129] It was demolished in 2001.

The Social Scene

The Palm Island Club was built by the Beach Construction Company in 1922 on the north shore of Palm Island, at the foot of the bridge to Hibiscus Island. Original owners were Locke Highleyman and gambler John Olive.[130] It was a private social club, and a dining room and kitchen were added in 1927. After Prohibition ended, it was remodeled as a nightclub by architect Russell Pancoast in 1934. Bouche's Villa Venice occupied it for a time, and in the 1950s, it became the Latin Quarter, run by Lou Walters. The building was demolished in 1968.

Club Lido, on the south shore of Hibiscus Island, across from the Palm Island Club, was a supper club like its New York counterpart, but during Prohibition, it was common knowledge that both this and the Palm Island

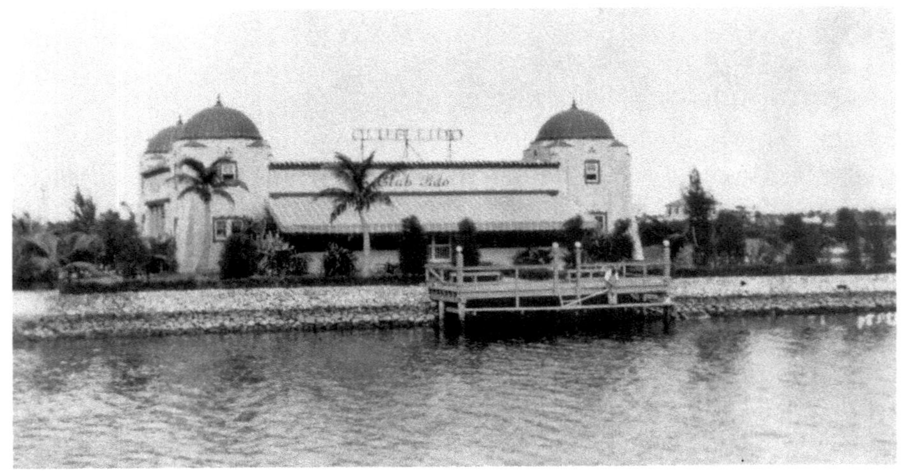

Club Lido, built in 1925 as a private social club on Hibiscus Island, later became the Rod and Reel Club. *Courtesy Arva Moore Parks,* Miami News *collection.*

Club were illegal gambling and drinking establishments. The Lido was built in twenty days at the beginning of 1925.[131] The two-story building cost over $24,000 and was designed by the local firm of Robertson & Patterson. Edwin L. Robertson came to Miami from Georgia in 1919 and worked with August Geiger; Lawrence R. Patterson went to the University of Pennsylvania, came here in 1915 and worked with Walter DeGarmo. The two formed a partnership in 1923.[132]

Framing the west and south façades of the Club Lido were three stocky, square towers topped with ribbed copper domes that were something of a landmark. The south side faced the water, and the entrance was on the west, with a front portico supported by four Tuscan-style columns.

The building had a second life as home to the Miami Beach Rod and Reel Club. This club was founded in 1929, with fifty members, both men and women, meeting first in the chamber of commerce building and later in a bayside clubhouse north of the Venetian Causeway. From its beginnings, the Rod & Reel Club combined social activities with a serious interest in fishing and conservation efforts. In 1934, with a membership of four hundred, the club moved into the Club Lido building. Since Prohibition was over, weekly meetings started with a cocktail hour and seafood dinner followed by a guest speaker or other informative programs on fishing. The club participated in fishing tournaments all over the world and often entertained visiting dignitaries, including the Duke of Windsor.

In 2009, the clubhouse was vacated because of escalating property taxes, and an effort to designate it as a historic site failed. Since the structure did not lend itself to the residential use required by zoning, it was demolished in 2011.

The LA GORCE GOLF CLUB was situated on the east side of Alton Road at Fifty-seventh Street. The clubhouse for the golf course of the same name was built by Carl Fisher Properties in 1927. Fisher had created the golf course with a million cubic yards of fill from the bay and named it for his friend John Oliver La Gorce, editor of the *National Geographic* magazine in Washington, D.C. Neither Fisher nor La Gorce played golf, but this was an amenity that attracted the wealthy who did. Fisher named the holes for eighteen of them. The club opened in January 1928 and, just two months later, held the first of four annual tournaments that attracted top golfers.

The grand two-story clubhouse was designed by August Geiger in the Mediterranean style with, of course, Beaux-Arts features such as urns, quoins, pilasters and stone scrolls and balustrades. The structure was U-shaped, embracing a courtyard on the west that was framed by two grand staircases leading to a second-floor balcony. Another balcony above a round-arched loggia faced the golf course on the east. The interior, with the dining room and ballroom on the second floor, featured a twin grand staircase with decorative iron railings, Corinthian columns and ornate ceilings.

In 1945, the five hundred members of the golf club purchased the facility and renamed it the La Gorce Country Club. In 1954, architect Roy F. France designed $300,000 worth of additions that filled in the original courtyard and obliterated many exterior features, but much of the interior remained intact. In July 2001, the city's Historic Preservation Board initiated the process to designate the building as a historic site, but before this could go into effect, the club's membership voted to demolish the building, and it fell in September.[133]

CHAPTER 8

LINCOLN ROAD

One would not expect to find a major thoroughfare named for Abraham Lincoln this far south, but Carl Fisher was from Indianapolis, and Lincoln was one of his heroes. In addition to his Prest-O-Lite company and Speedway projects in Indiana, in 1912, Fisher began a campaign to construct the Lincoln Highway, the nation's first coast-to-coast auto route. It linked New York to San Francisco and was mostly completed by 1915. In 1914, Fisher started planning a similar project, the Dixie Highway, that would connect Chicago and Michigan to Miami, where he was creating an ocean-side resort he called Alton Beach on his newly acquired land.

By the time the town of Miami Beach was incorporated in 1915, there were three major developers here: the Lummus brothers at the south end of the peninsula up to about Fifteenth Street; the Collins-Pancoast family north of Nineteenth Street; and Carl Fisher, who started with the land in between. Howard Kleinberg describes their different goals:

> *Lummus' Ocean Beach Realty was working toward a residential community of modest means, with small hotels for visitors. The Collins family seemed more interested in attracting well-to-do persons anticipating a quiet retreat on the beach, much as was happening just north in Palm Beach. Fisher was after the new young lions of American industry—colleagues in the automotive world and others who had recently come upon their fortunes and loved to spend their dollars on fast boats and cars, polo ponies and*

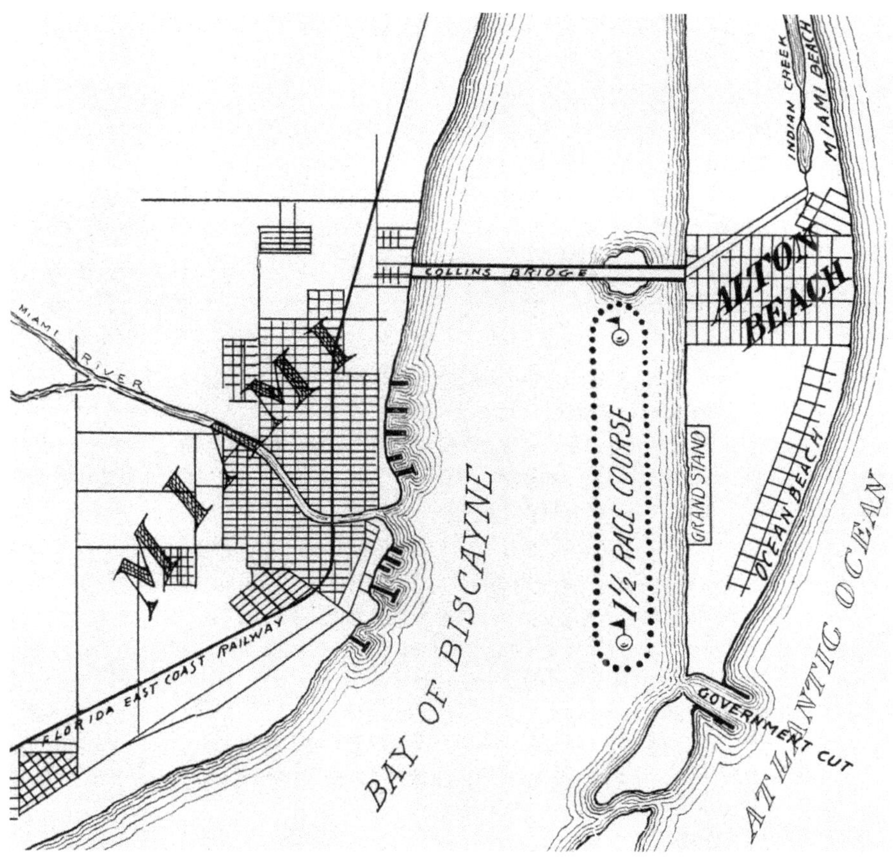

Miami Beach was not yet a town when the Alton Beach Realty Company produced this map in 1914, and the Collins Bridge was the only link across Biscayne Bay. Alton Beach was Carl Fisher's land; he put Lincoln Road across the middle of it and organized boat-racing regattas in the bay. To the south was the Lummus brothers' Ocean Beach and to the north, the Collins-Pancoast family called their development Miami Beach. *Courtesy City of Miami Beach Historical Archive.*

> *ostentatious parties that he didn't like to attend. Both Collins and Fisher envisioned several grand hotels.*[134]

The 200 acres that John Collins gave Fisher in January 1913, plus another 105 acres he got from J.N. Lummus in March, became Fishers First Subdivision (there would be many more to come). His Alton Beach Realty Company platted it on January 15, 1914, and Fisher laid out Lincoln Road from east to west through the center of it. First, the dense mangrove forest had to be cleared, but within a decade, Lincoln Road became the cultural and commercial center of Miami Beach, with homes, hotels, sports facilities, a movie theater and a school among its earliest buildings that are now lost.

FISHER'S HOME AND OFFICE

Fisher first built his own residence at the east end of Lincoln Road, at 1616 Ocean Drive, late in 1914. It stood directly on the beach, far back from Collins Avenue, and faced the ocean. Building materials for the house were brought in by barge because the last link of the Collins Bridge from Belle Isle had not been entirely completed by then.[135] Many sources attribute this house to August Geiger, who designed many of Fisher's projects. No official building records survive, but two newspapers at the time instead name the architect of the house as GEORGE L. PFEIFFER.[136] Born and educated in Germany, Pfeiffer first came to the United States to work on the German pavilion at the 1893 Chicago World's Fair and settled there for a while but moved to Miami for his health in 1909. J.N. Lummus took Pfeiffer out of

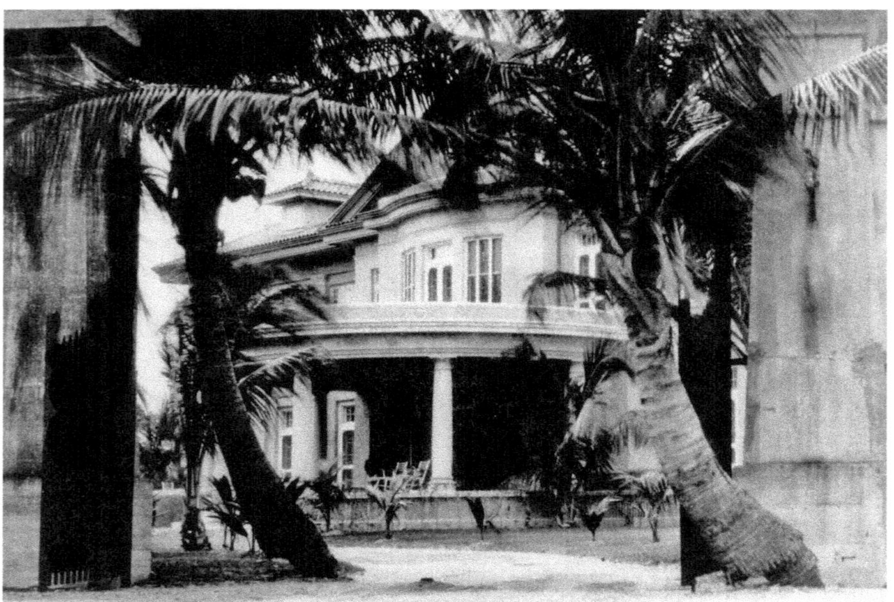

Carl and Jane Fisher's home, The Shadows, fronting the ocean at the head of Lincoln Road, was built in 1914 as one of the earliest homes on the beach. *Courtesy Arva Moore Parks.*

retirement in 1910 to design commercial buildings in Miami,[137] and he maintained an active practice here until his death in 1938. August Geiger designed Carl Fisher's second Miami Beach house on North Bay Road in 1925, which may be the source of the confusion.

Fisher's Lincoln Road house was an elegant estate in an austere Italian Renaissance style. A distinctive rounded portico with Tuscan columns faced the ocean, and an abundance of palm trees made the home's name, The Shadows, appropriate. On the first floor were an immense living room, a drawing room, a library, a dining room, a kitchen and a butler's pantry. On the second floor were the master bedroom and three others, each with its own bath. The third-floor level was used for entertaining, with an enclosed roof garden and ballroom.[138] Fisher and his wife, Jane, lived in the house for about ten years and entertained many illustrious guests here, including Will Rogers, Irving Berlin and James Whitcomb Riley. Jane gave this description of the house in her book *Fabulous Hoosier*:

> *The Shadows, when finally complete, was enchanting, spacious and cool. The green lawn and the moving Atlantic seemed to enter the 300 square feet of ceiling-high window frontage and become part of the immense drawing-room with its sea-green carpets and large sofas and chairs lushly padded with down and covered with pale green cotton damask. One came down a curved twin stairway, framed with the golden tubes of the pipe organ, into these wide, beautiful rooms that held the serenity of the garden and the sea. Cypress logs burned in the fireplaces…* [which were] *large enough for* [Carl] *to "walk into and turn around." Final touches in the house were two immense brass cuspidors…That house was Florida. Even the table china I ordered from Lenox was made with an orange-tree design, and our silver bore the same device.*[139]

Fisher's home soon inspired his wealthy friends to build their own winter homes nearby. A 1915 photograph shows a house under construction just north of Fisher's; it was built for John H. Hanan of New York, but by 1921, it had become the residence of Frank A. Seiberling. He co-founded the Goodyear Tire and Rubber Company of Akron, Ohio, in 1898 and had been one of the investors in Fisher's Lincoln Highway project. The distinguished Beaux-Arts mansion, when finished, had a porch with two-story Corinthian columns facing the ocean, quoins along its edges and a stone balustrade around its parapet.

The photo also shows a tennis court at this early stage of Lincoln Road. It was one of many sports—golf, polo, motorboat racing—that Fisher would

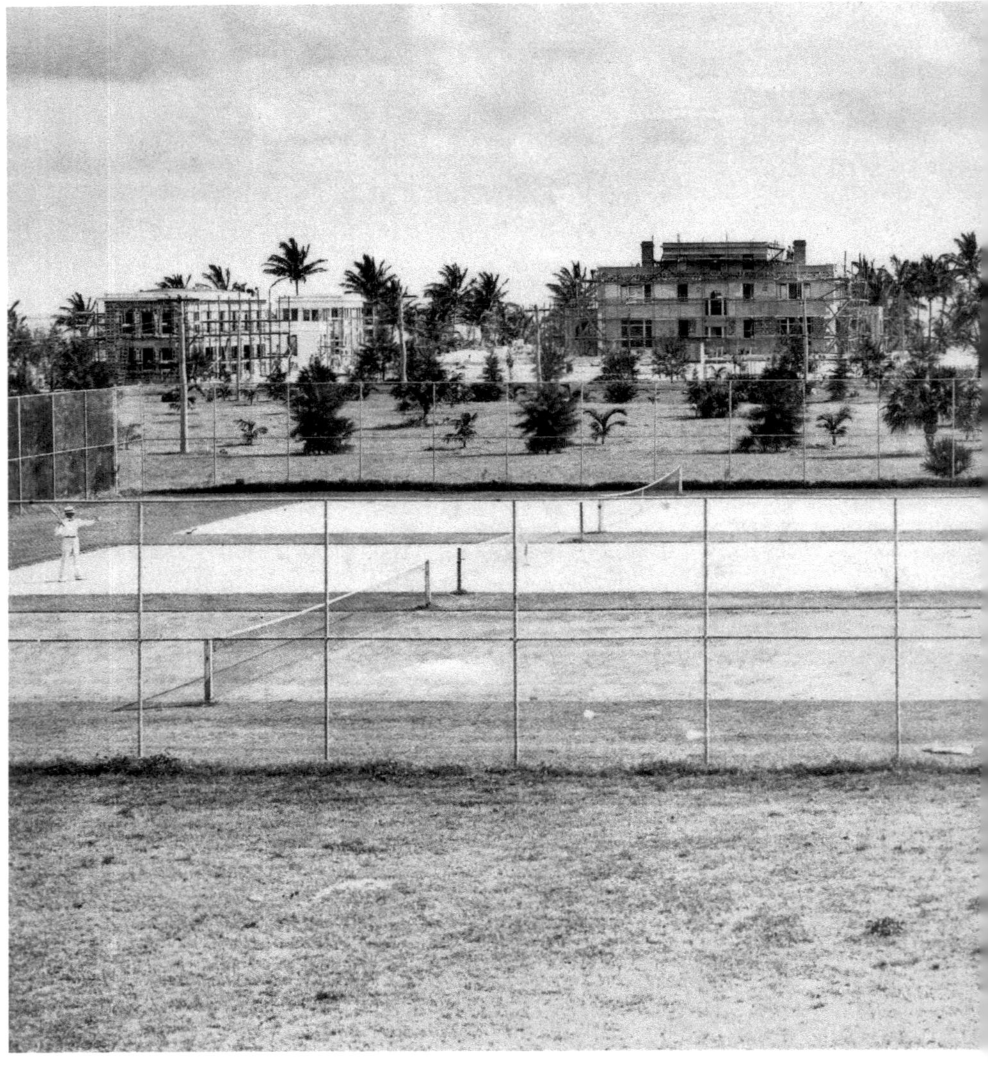

The east end of Lincoln Road in 1915. The rear of the Fisher residence is at right; the house under construction at center was later owned by tire magnate Frank Seiberling. *Courtesy City of Miami Beach Historical Archive.*

promote in order to attract a young, active crowd to Miami Beach. In 1917, August Geiger designed an enclosed tennis court to the north of the surface courts, on the north side of Lincoln Road between James and Washington Avenues. It was lighted, so one could play day or night.

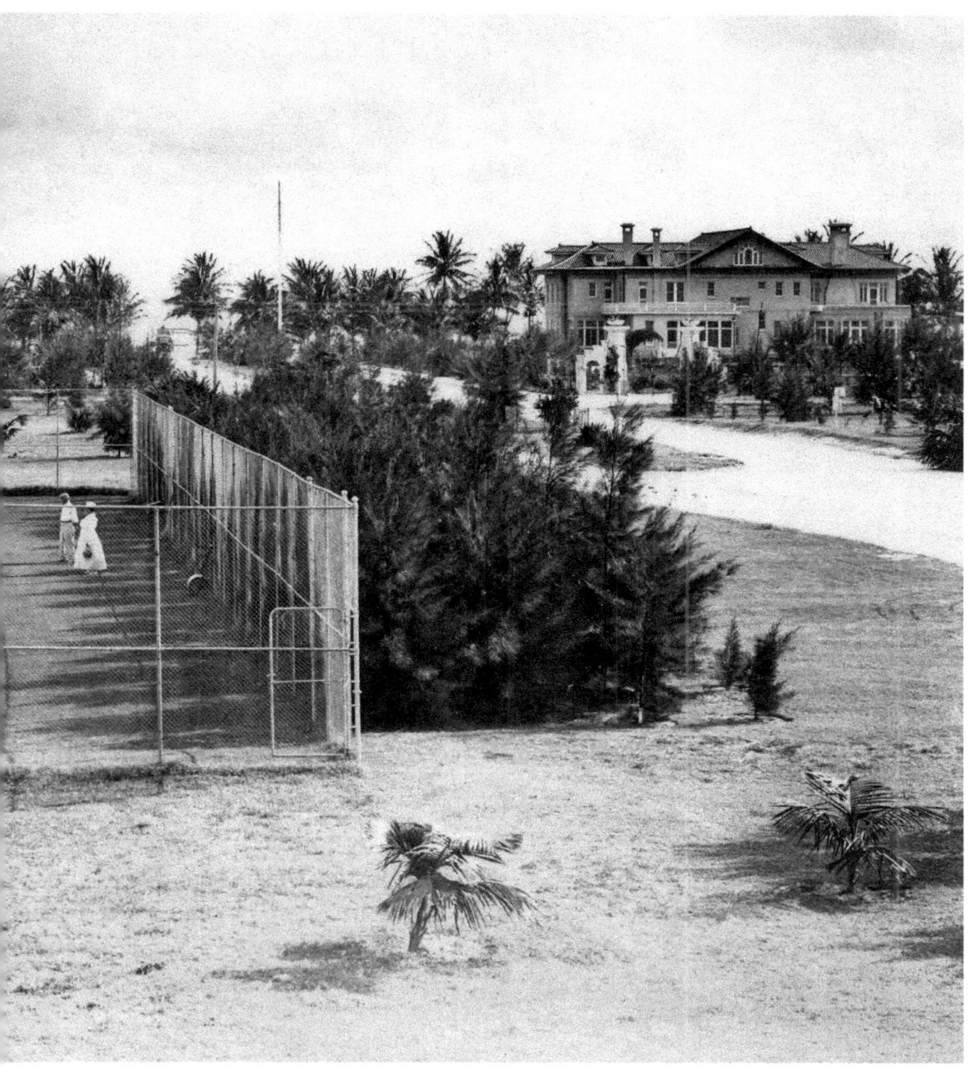

Also built prior to 1918 was the Alton Beach Realty Company's own office, a sturdy, two-story Italian Renaissance–style building on the northeast corner of Lincoln Road and Washington Avenue, which was then called Miami Avenue. (It was Fisher who renamed some of the avenues of Miami Beach after counterparts in Indianapolis.) This handsome structure had heavy moldings, classic pediments and softly arched French doors opening onto two front balconies with stone balustrades.

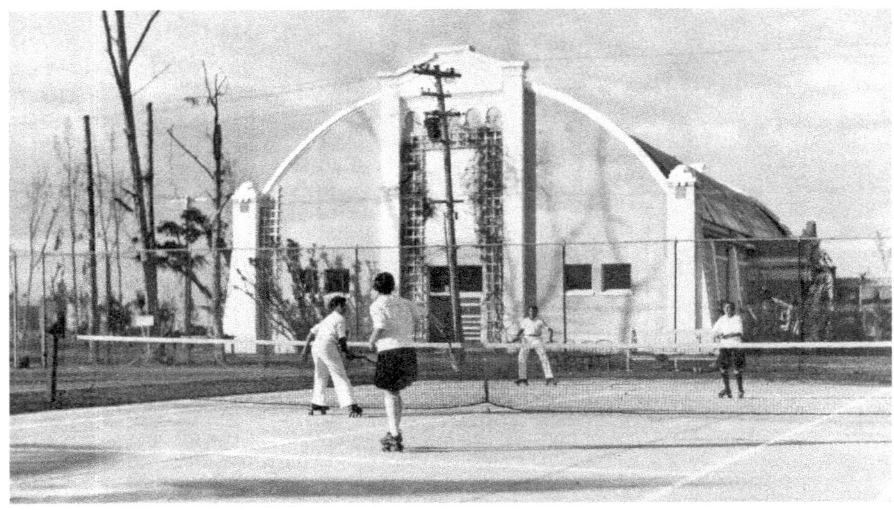

August Geiger designed this indoor tennis court on the north side of Lincoln Road in 1917. One could also play tennis on roller skates. *Courtesy City of Miami Beach Historical Archive.*

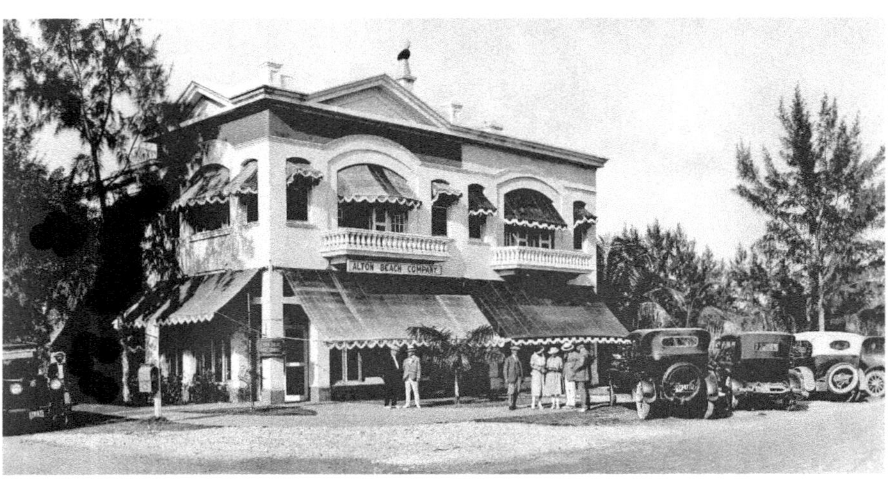

The office for Fisher's Alton Beach Realty Company stood on the northeast corner of Lincoln Road and Washington Avenue, seen here in 1924. *Courtesy City of Miami Beach Historical Archive.*

In 1923, Alton Beach Realty built another two-story office building immediately north of this one, at 1657 Washington Avenue (the name had changed by then). This housed the engineering department of the Carl Fisher interests on the first floor and Thomas Pancoast's office for the

Miami Beach Improvement Company upstairs. It was designed by Kiehnel & Elliott in the Mediterranean style, with a flat roof, Mission-style parapet and baroque door surround.[140]

In August 1924, Fisher completed a new seven-story office building for himself that still stands on Lincoln Road at Jefferson Avenue. August Geiger designed it, and it was renamed the Van Dyke Building for its new owner in 1937. When Fisher's realty company moved over there, both of the former office buildings became an annex to Fisher's Lincoln Hotel, which was diagonally across the street. When the Lincoln was torn down in 1940, they remained as the Annex Hotel, with eighteen rooms. They were demolished in 1951.

In 1925, Fisher's marriage failed, and he sold his oceanfront property from Fifteenth to Twentieth Streets, including The Shadows, to Newton B.T. Roney, whom we met in Chapter 4. The Shadows eventually became a notorious gambling house known as the Beach and Tennis Club and later the Lincoln Manor Restaurant. It was finally demolished about 1960 for the construction of the One Hundred Lincoln Road Apartments, later known as Decoplage.

OTHER HOMES

A photograph taken from the roof of the Alton Beach Realty office looking southward in June 1924 shows the residential nature of this area at that time: it was a neighborhood of estates, and the picture shows four of them on the south side of Lincoln Road between Collins and Washington Avenues, amid a forest of palm trees and Australian pines.

At the far right in this photo, at 1625 Washington Avenue, is the towered, Mediterranean-style home of Elliott F. Shepard, built in 1923 at the cost of $48,000 (equivalent to over $600,000 in 2014), architect unknown. Shepard, grandson of Cornelius Vanderbilt, was a "sportsman, yachtsman and millionaire" who, with his wife, Eleanor, had lived in France before coming to Florida around 1922. During World War I, they gave their French chateau for hospital use, working there themselves. Shepard received the Croix de Guerre and Legion of Honor from the French government and died at his Washington Avenue home, called La Terradella, in 1927.[141]

The other three houses in the photo were built for Fred J. Osius (1879–ca. 1935), founder of the Hamilton Beach appliance company of Racine,

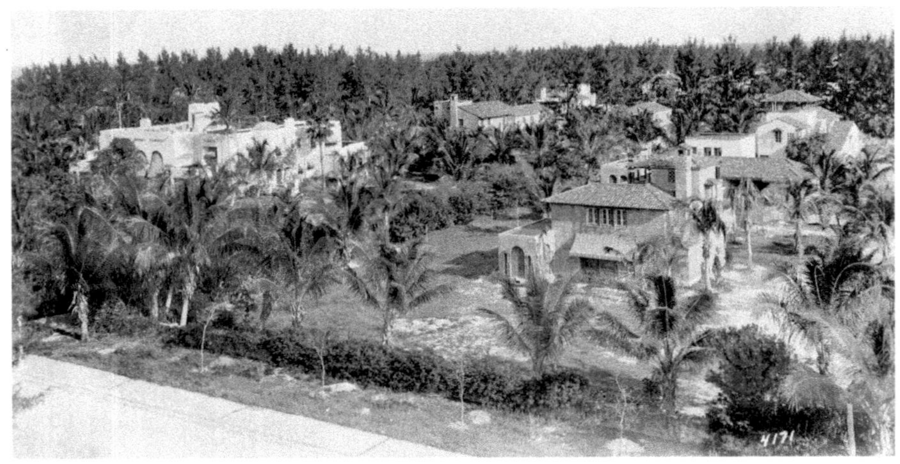

The view from the roof of the Alton Beach Realty building in June 1924 shows the south side of Lincoln Road between Collins and Washington Avenues when this was a residential neighborhood. *Courtesy HistoryMiami, Claude Matlack Collection 91-2.*

Wisconsin. Osius himself invented a drink mixer that evolved into the familiar blender. He sold his company and moved to Florida in 1922, becoming a prominent developer in Miami and Miami Beach with the Osius Realty Company. The house at the lower right in the picture was his own residence at 1627 Washington Avenue. The house in the distance, at 1610 Collins Avenue, was purchased by William J. Morris, a steel industrialist from Pittsburgh, who named it Bienvenida. Both of these houses were built in 1923 and designed in the Mediterranean style by the Pittsburgh firm of Kiehnel & Elliott, with Richard Kiehnel at the helm of the Miami office.

The fourth house, seen at the left, is the most fascinating. Costing $72,000 (comparable to $1.016 million in 2014), it was built at 230 Lincoln Road in 1922, designed by the Philadelphia architectural firm of McLanahan & Bencker. This firm had started as the venerable Price & McLanahan, and Ralph B. Bencker (1883–1961) had supervised its Indianapolis office since 1904. Price & McLanahan leaned toward the Arts and Crafts style, but after William Price's death in 1916, Bencker brought in a Moderne influence;[142] his first employer, Paul Davis, had studied in Paris, where Moderne, or Art Deco, was well underway long before the 1925 Exposition that showcased it. Another photo of this boxy, two-story house shows more detail: tall, ornamented arched windows and strips of bas-relief at the parapet. It was probably the first Art Deco building in Miami Beach and way ahead of its time.

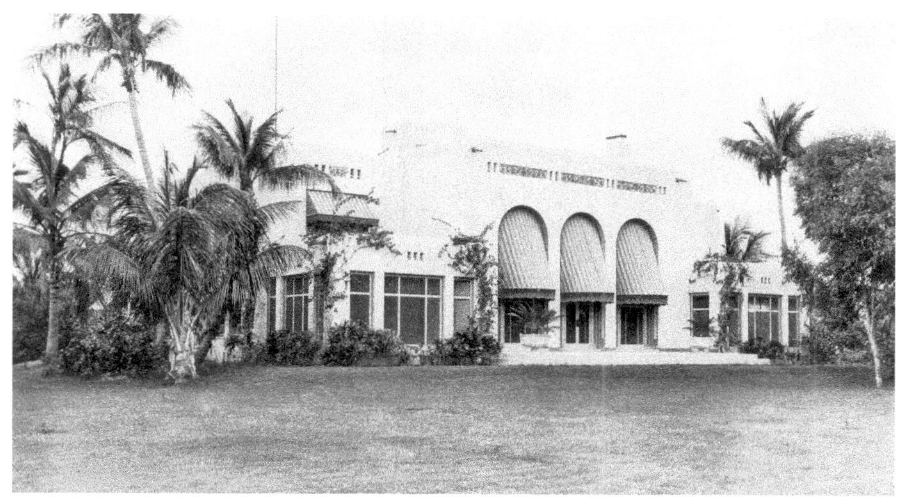

One of the houses in the previous photo, at 230 Lincoln Road. Designed by McLanahan & Bencker in 1922, it was probably the earliest Moderne, or Art Deco, building in Miami Beach. *Courtesy HistoryMiami, Claude Matlack Collection 94-2.*

All of these houses met their demise due to zoning changes. As mentioned above, Newton Roney bought the east end of Lincoln Road from Carl Fisher in 1925. By the 1930s, the zoning here allowed hotels and apartment buildings, but in 1940, the Roney family sued the city to change the zoning to commercial use, arguing that "the character of the neighborhood had changed since the creation of the subdivision."[143] The suit was successful and, in 1946, the first to go was the Art Deco estate, which occupied more than eight building lots. The store building that L. Murray Dixon designed at the corner of Collins Avenue replaced it. The Morris house became an annex to the new Berkeley Shore Hotel in 1940 but was demolished ten years later. The Shepard house fell in 1948. Parts of the Osius residence were torn down in 1948; other parts were remodeled into apartments, and in 1950, Osius's widow, Louise, added storefronts along Washington Avenue, where she herself operated Louise's Beauty Salon.

West of Washington Avenue

In 1916, Fisher completed a 120-acre municipal golf course extending north from Lincoln Road between Washington and Meridian Avenues; in 1920, it was narrowed to Euclid Avenue, which dead-ends at Lincoln Road. A bridle path ran along the western border of the golf course. The first nine holes were south of the Collins Canal, where the clubhouse was built (designed by August Geiger), and the second half of the course was north of the canal. The attraction was that guests at Fisher's Lincoln Hotel could just walk out the door and be at the first tee. Today, with an unbroken line of buildings along Lincoln Road, it is hard to imagine how open it once was.

In 1935, commercial buildings were first allowed along the north side of Lincoln Road, across from the Lincoln Hotel, in the two blocks between Washington and Euclid Avenues. The Lincoln Theatre, the "605 Lincoln Road Building" and a store building by Russell Pancoast, all still standing, were built soon thereafter. One building that was lost was a little domed bank building, a landmark at the corner of Washington Avenue. It opened on January 22, 1940, designed by Roy F. France in the Art Deco style for the Miami Beach Federal Savings and Loan Association. It was only one story but reached a height of twenty-three feet. It was demolished in 1955 and replaced by the present, larger bank. Behind these buildings, most of the golf course remained intact until after World War II; in fact, it was used as a drill field by the recruits in training here during the war. The city had

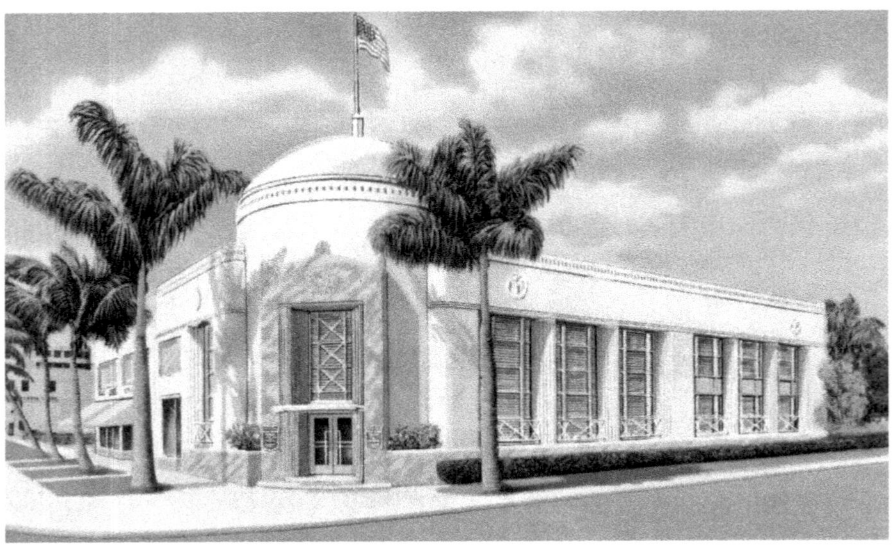

This little domed building for the Miami Beach Federal Savings and Loan Company, designed by Roy F. France in 1939, was a landmark on Lincoln Road at Washington Avenue. *Postcard courtesy of Larry Wiggins.*

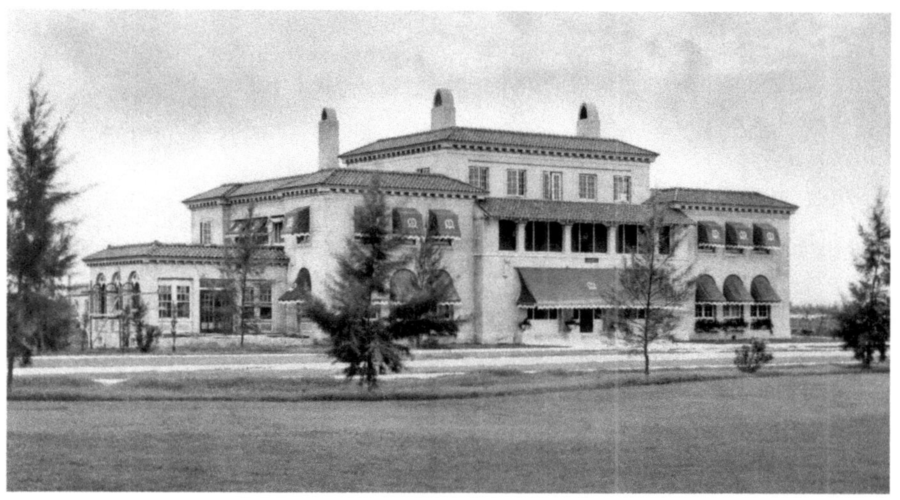

The Lincoln Apartments, designed by August Geiger in 1917. *Courtesy Arva Moore Parks.*

bought the golf course from Fisher and, in later years, built the Miami Beach Auditorium, the Convention Center and city hall on it as public land.

This brings us to the Lincoln Hotel, the first of Carl Fisher's five Miami Beach hotels. The Lincoln would occupy the whole block between Washington and Drexel Avenues on the south side of Lincoln Road, but it was built in two parts. The Lincoln Apartments (which also had hotel rooms), designed by August Geiger, was begun in January 1917 at the west end of the block, and in 1919, the adjoining Lincoln Hotel was constructed at the east end of the block. There is more about the Lincoln Hotel in Chapter 9.

We met August Geiger on Millionaires' Row. Besides three homes there, Geiger designed many of Carl Fisher's projects, some surviving and some not. Though his Lincoln Apartments building was Mediterranean in style, Geiger, like many architects of his time, was trained in the Beaux-Arts tradition. This originated in the École des Beaux-Arts (School of Fine Arts) in Paris. The school's approach to architecture in the late nineteenth century had tremendous influence in Europe and America and was the chief style of the Chicago World's Fair in 1893. It was based on Classical rules of scale, proportion and symmetry but embellished the structures with a French flair using decorative shields, crests, swags, garlands, urns, quoins, bas-relief panels, statuary, et cetera.[144] It was, in a word, pretty. Beaux-Arts was not only a style in itself but also exerted an influence on other styles. Carl Fisher seemed to love it, at least for public buildings.

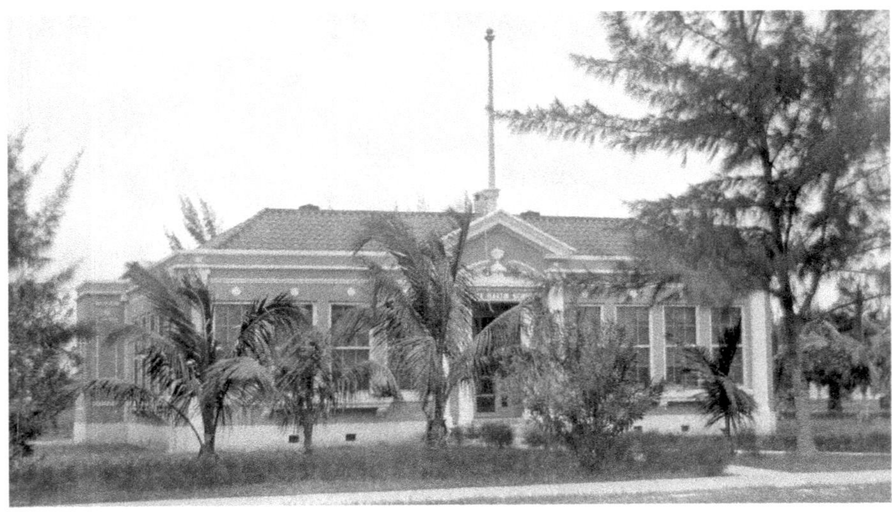

The Eunice Martin School was built at the northwest corner of Lincoln Road and Jefferson Avenue in 1919. A few years later, it was moved onto Michigan Avenue. *Postcard courtesy of HistoryMiami.*

The building contractor for most of Carl Fisher's Miami Beach projects was Cecil B. Floyd, whom Fisher brought from Indianapolis. Floyd graduated from Purdue University in 1907. He built Fisher's Prest-O-Lite plants in Indianapolis and twenty-seven other cities and came to Miami Beach in 1919. Here he founded the Beach Construction Company, which became the largest industrial enterprise in the city.[145] Besides many private residences, his company's projects included the aquarium and chamber of commerce buildings on Fifth Street; the Flamingo Hotel; and the Altonia Hotel, Community Theatre and First National Bank on Lincoln Road.

One of the projects completed by Fisher in 1919 was the Eunice Martin School, built on the northwest corner of Lincoln Road and Jefferson Avenue. Fisher would build the city's first public school the next year, but at this time, Miami Beach children either attended private schools or traveled across the bay to public schools in Miami. No building records survive, but this charming little one-story Beaux-Arts schoolhouse must have been August Geiger's work; he was a longtime designer of schools, starting with public schools in the towns of Homestead, Arch Creek and Dania prior to 1914.[146]

This building had an interesting history. In 1921, the newspaper reported that the headmistress of the Montmare School, a girls' boarding school housed at the Pancoast estate at that time, would also be conducting a day school at "the school on Lincoln Road formerly under Miss Eunice Martin."[147] A few years later, the school building was moved around the corner to 1673 Michigan Avenue, about half a block north of Lincoln Road, and was converted to a residence. The reason for this was explained by C.W. "Pete" Chase Jr., who was Carl Fisher's sales manager. He said that after Fisher built his seven-story office building in 1924, he "decided he was really going to make Lincoln Road into a high-class shopping street," and he didn't think it was an appropriate place for a school.[148] In 1928, Russell Pancoast designed the Mead Building where the school had been.

The next chapter of its story came after the 1926 hurricane. As you may recall from Chapter 7, the Committee of One Hundred was a local civic group formed in 1926, with author Clayton Sedgwick Cooper as president. Pete Chase continued:

> *Clayton Cooper had owned a little home directly on the ocean front, along about Thirty-eighth Street. It was a small wooden house, and the 1926 hurricane just took that house apart and there was never a sign of any part of it when the storm was over. Cooper lost all of his personal effects, his very fine library, his furnishings;—everything that was in there. He had no home and Mr. Fisher wanted to help the Committee of One Hundred to keep going, so he permitted Clayton and Mrs. Cooper to live in this schoolhouse that had been moved and changed over into a residence—that was the building Cooper felt should be the Committee's Club House. Carl Fisher had given this property to Mrs. Fisher and, at a very fair price and on liberal terms, the Committee purchased it from her.*

The Committee of One Hundred bought the building from Jane Fisher in 1932, when the committee's membership had grown to three hundred and its meeting room next to the bank on Alton Road was too small. It used this building as its headquarters for nineteen years, from 1932 to 1951, and added an auditorium, designed by August Geiger, in 1938. In 1951, the city council bought the property, and it was torn down to make room for parking.[149] The Committee of One Hundred, as we have seen, then moved into more luxurious digs at the Adams estate on Belle Isle.

THE COMMUNITY THEATRE

In 1920, Carl Fisher began to construct a theater, the Altonia, at the northwest corner of Lincoln Road and Michigan Avenue, but he got only as far as the foundations.

On December 18, 1922, a number of prominent Miami Beach residents met to form the Miami Beach Community Theatre Corporation for the purpose of building a movie theater. President of the group was Chicago publisher William F. Whitman; other participants included Miami Beach mayor Louis Snedigar, Thomas Pancoast, Jane Fisher and architect Martin L. Hampton, who was chosen to design the project.[150] It was financed by offering twenty-five thousand shares in the company at $10 per share. Fisher took $25,000 worth of stock in exchange for the site, and the Community Theatre was built on the foundations he had laid for the Altonia. Public sale of shares made this truly a community effort:

> *Probably no building under construction at Miami Beach…carries in its building half the interest of the Community theatre. Here is a building which the people have subscribed to and which the people will own…It is destined to be a place of great pride to the people of this city.*[151]

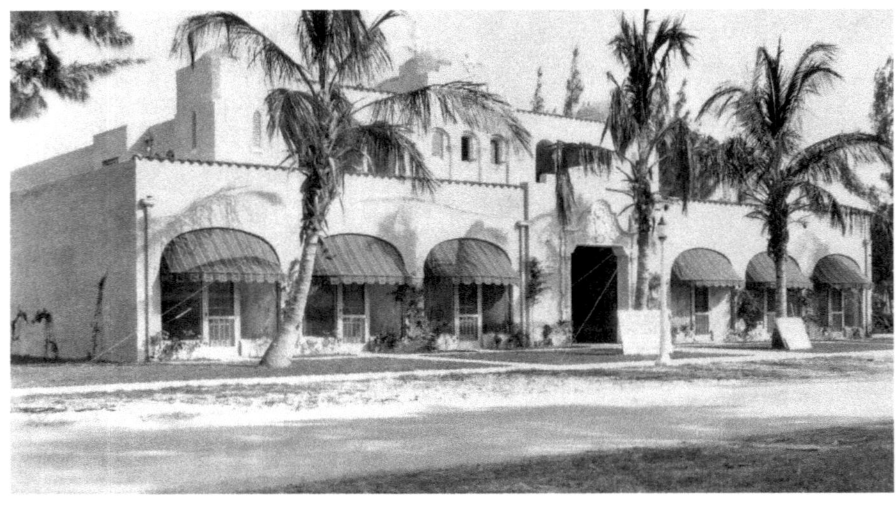

The Community Theatre, designed by Martin L. Hampton in 1923, was Miami Beach's first movie theater, at the northwest corner of Lincoln Road and Michigan Avenue. *Courtesy City of Miami Beach Historical Archive.*

Hampton designed a truly impressive building in the Spanish Colonial Revival style. From the beginning, it included retail space in addition to the theater; six rounded arches on Lincoln Road and three on Michigan Avenue defined the one-story storefronts. The theater was a two-story structure rising behind them, with a grand Spanish Baroque entrance and decorated with cast-stone urns, scrolling, ornamental columns and a trio of domes on the roof. The seven-hundred-seat auditorium was intended mostly to be a movie theater, but it also had a stage, four dressing rooms and an orchestra pit for musical performances, as well as a good-quality organ to accompany the films, which were silent.

The Community Theatre was leased by Paramount and opened on Sunday, December 23, 1923, with the film *Rosita*, starring Mary Pickford. It was Miami Beach's first cinema.

During World War II, the theater was one of hundreds of Miami Beach buildings leased by the U.S. Army Air Forces training command. It served as a classroom for lectures and training films for the thousands of recruits posted here. It returned to civilian use in 1944, but just ten years later, the auditorium portion of the Community Theatre was demolished. The storefronts remained and expanded into the former theater space, but after many remodels, what was left of the building had lost its original splendor long before it was demolished in 2014.

Commercial Buildings

At the other end of this block, at the northeast corner of Lenox Avenue, another lost building went up in 1925. Originally called the Lincoln Road Building, it was designed by John Bullen (1898–1948),[152] an architect from Wisconsin who designed many homes and commercial buildings here in the 1920s. Extensive remodeling by an unidentified architect took place in 1929. The distinctive feature of this one-story retail building was its façade of softly pointed arches, supported by ornate columns, which defined the storefronts along both streets. These arches and columns were covered over in stucco when the building was remodeled as the McAllister Building in 1938. Forty years later, the building was acquired by the South Florida Art Center, a project headed by preservation architect Randall Sender. After his death in 1990, the building was dedicated to him and again renamed as the Sender Building. Another renovation in 1998 removed the stucco from the

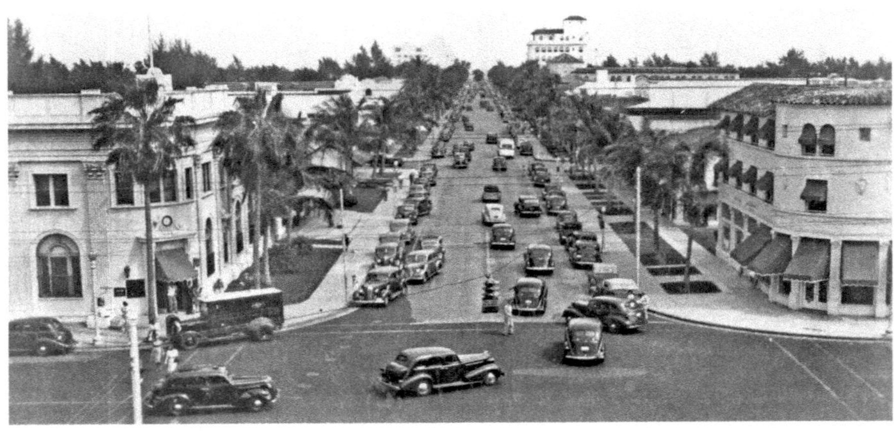

Looking east down Lincoln Road from Alton Road in the 1930s. At left is the Miami Beach First National Bank, designed by H. George Fink; at right is the Altonia Hotel. The tall building in the distance was Carl Fisher's office building, still standing at Jefferson Avenue. *Courtesy of Arva Moore Parks.*

original arches and columns, but in May 1999, the outer walls collapsed due to failure of structural supports. The new building on the site imitates some of the original design elements.

Since 1960, most of Lincoln Road has been a pedestrian mall that Fontainebleau Hotel architect Morris Lapidus designed, but this was originally a street open to automobile traffic. The accompanying photograph looks east at the intersection of Lincoln Road and Alton Road in the 1930s. At left is the imposing Miami Beach First National Bank, the first bank in Miami Beach. H. George Fink designed it in 1922 in the Neoclassical style.[153]

HENRY GEORGE FINK (1891–1975) was born in Pennsylvania and was the cousin of Coral Gables developer George E. Merrick. His family moved to Miami in 1904, and H. George graduated from Miami High School in 1907. He studied architecture at the Drexel Institute and at the University of Pennsylvania, then returned to Miami and worked with August Geiger. Between 1915 and 1921, Fink designed several of Carl Fisher's projects in Miami Beach, including the Ida Fisher Elementary School. In 1921, he and Martin Hampton became the first architects of George Merrick's Coral Gables. Like Hampton, Fink traveled to Spain to study the architecture there. It was Fink who coined the term "Mediterranean" in 1923 to describe the new architectural style in Florida, and he never added "Revival" to it.

At right in this photo is the Altonia Hotel, which John Bullen designed in 1925, the same year as his other building at Lenox Avenue. The three-story, Mediterranean-style Altonia cost $75,000 and had forty-four guest rooms, as well as ground-floor retail space. Its rounded corner echoed that of the bank across the street, and it was ornamented with fancy pilasters and decorative shields. In the 1920s, there were three hotels on Lincoln Road: the Altonia; the Hampton, which became an office building and still stands at Michigan Avenue; and, of course, the Lincoln.

The Altonia Hotel was demolished in 1969. A movie multiplex stands on the site today.

Chapter 9

The Carl Fisher Hotels

Carl Fisher was primarily interested in selling his land to create a community of wealthy winter residents. His approach was to build up a property, sell it at cost or borrow against it and then go build another. As Fisher wrote to a prospective client in 1921 concerning the Lincoln and Flamingo Hotels:

> *Primarily we are in the land business. If we can sell either of these high grade hotels, we wish to do so even though we receive less than their actual cost of construction. When these hotels are sold we will build others and sell them under the same conditions. We need at least twenty hotels of 150 room capacity each at Miami Beach.*[154]

As he built more amenities, his land values rose. As he dredged up the bay to make it navigable, he literally created more real estate. He was not in the hotel business, and yet he built five wonderful hotels here.

The Lincoln Hotel

The Lincoln Hotel would eventually cover the whole block between Washington and Drexel Avenues on the south side of Lincoln Road, but the western part was built first, in 1916, as the Lincoln Apartments. It opened

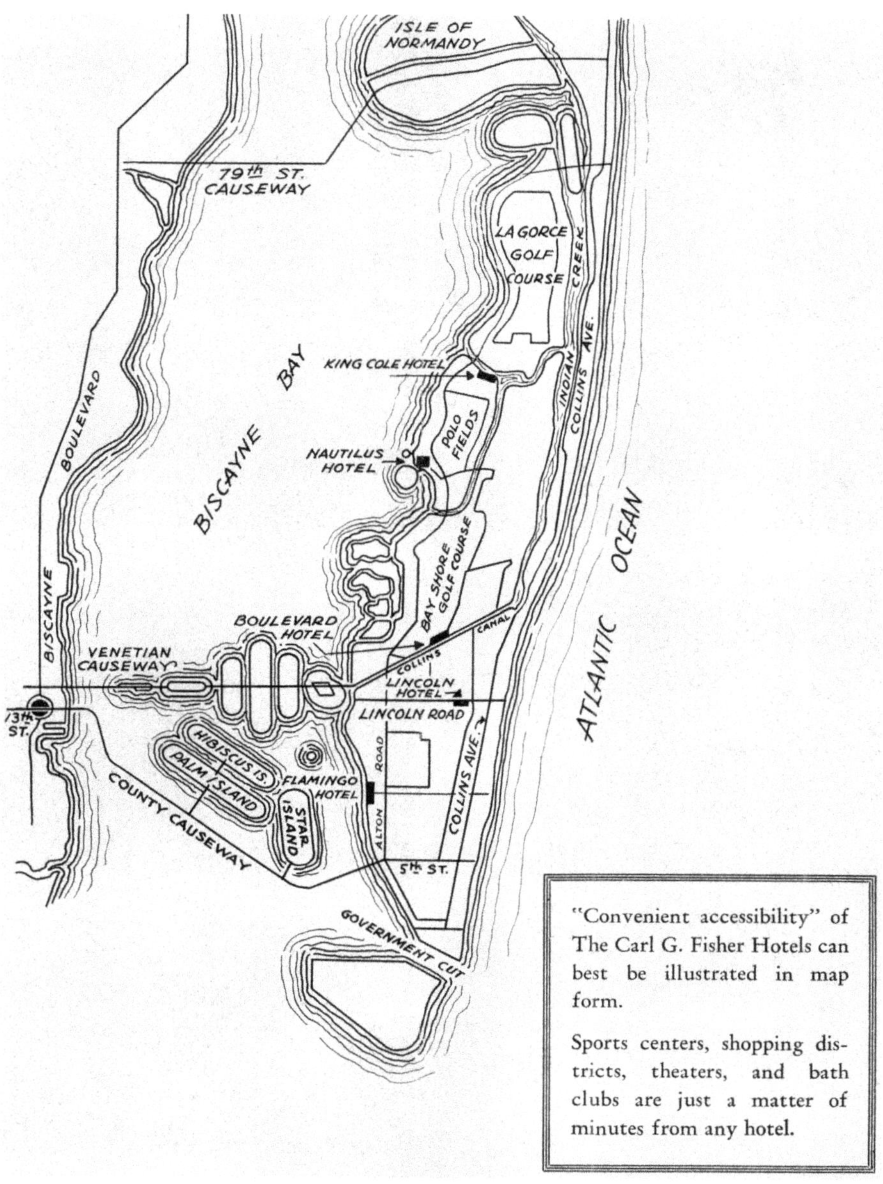

This 1930s promotional map for the Carl G. Fisher Hotels shows the locations of all five of them. Compared to the 1914 map on page 93, the Venetian Causeway has replaced the Collins Bridge; many islands have been dredged from the bay bottom; the County Causeway opened in 1920 and the Seventy-ninth Street Causeway followed in 1929. *Courtesy City of Miami Beach Historical Archive.*

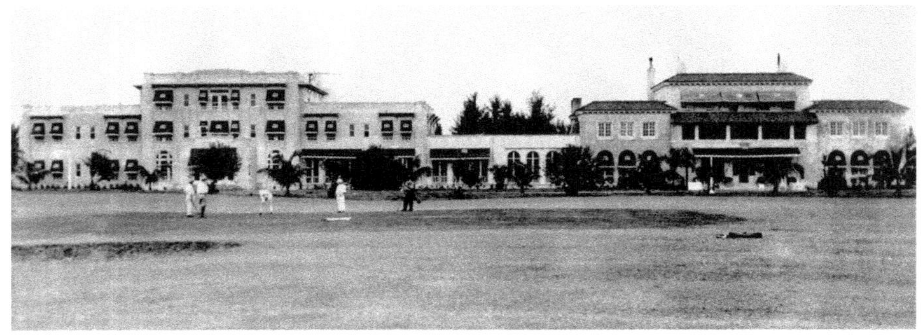

The Lincoln Hotel in 1920, with its new addition at left, faced the golf course. *Courtesy City of Miami Beach Historical Archive.*

on January 20, 1917, with twelve two-bedroom units that had no kitchens; there was a dining room on the ground floor for all meals. The building cost $40,000 and was designed by August Geiger.[155] The building had two-story wings on either side of the three-story center section and all had hip roofs of clay tile. The entrance had three round arches, and a screened porch was above it on the second floor.

The east addition was done in 1919. It had the same configuration of two- and three-story sections, but its roof was flat, and its general appearance was Italian Renaissance; it may have had a different architect. The two parts of the Lincoln were joined by a one-story section with rounded arches. The entire structure cost about $300,000 and had a total of sixty-six rooms.[156] The Lincoln conveyed a feeling of quiet refinement:

> *The Lincoln has been designed with the idea of providing its guests with every conceivable comfort. A building especially adapted to the requirements of the tropics—ample public rooms, spacious porches, large cheerful bedchambers luxuriously furnished, beautiful grounds and a real homelike atmosphere.*[157]

The Lincoln was demolished in 1940 for the construction of the Mercantile Bank Building at 420 Lincoln Road.[158]

THE FLAMINGO HOTEL

Opening officially on December 31, 1920, the Flamingo Hotel stood on the edge of the bay at the end of Fifteenth Street, two blocks south of Lincoln Road. It had side wings to the north and south of a center tower that rose to eleven stories and then was topped by a glass dome that added another thirty feet, making the Flamingo, at 154 feet, the second-tallest hotel in Florida in 1920 (the tallest being in Jacksonville).[159] At night, the dome was lit from within in constantly changing colors and could be seen for miles at sea.

The Flamingo has been attributed by various authors to two different architectural firms: Price & McLanahan of Philadelphia and Rubush & Hunter of Indianapolis. In her book, Polly Redford clears up the confusion. Fisher and Allison at first hired "a firm of fancy Philadelphia architects" to draw up plans, but they were too expensive even when the $750,000 budget was raised to $1 million. Allison then gave up the project, and Fisher "went to Indianapolis architects for cheaper designs."[160] So both firms drew plans for a Flamingo Hotel, but the Rubush & Hunter design was the one that materialized. (As you may recall from Chapter 3, Allison had hired Price & McLanahan to design the interior of his mansion in Indianapolis a few years earlier. Although Price died in 1916, the firm kept his name until 1919.)

The Flamingo was furnished by Wanamaker's, and the lobby was decorated with plaster bas-reliefs of flamingoes and a painting of the birds that was

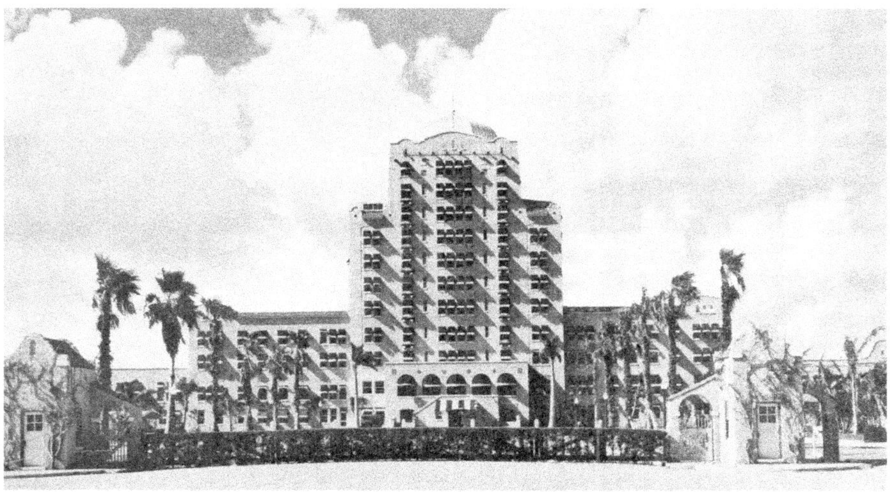

The Flamingo Hotel, on the bay at Fifteenth Street, opened on the last day of 1920. *Courtesy Arva Moore Parks.*

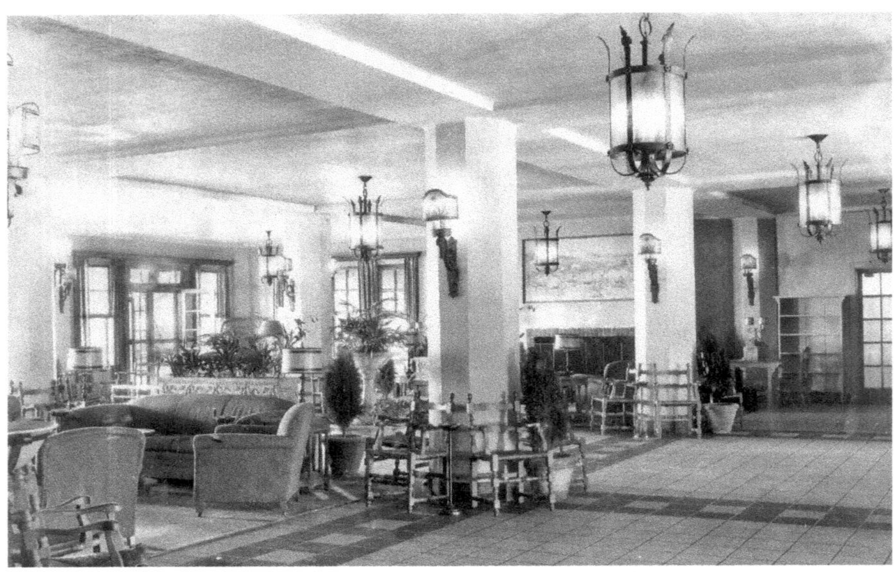

Lobby of the Flamingo Hotel, with a mural of flamingoes by Louis Fuertes. *Courtesy Arva Moore Parks, Pete Chase collection.*

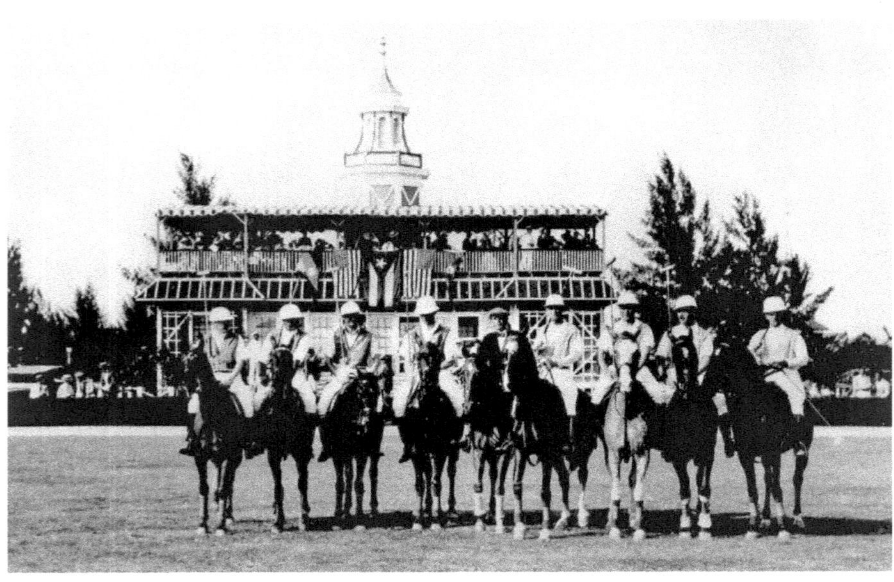

Cuban and American polo teams and the grandstand south of Lincoln Road. The Flamingo Hotel's sports fields became today's Flamingo Park. *Courtesy City of Miami Beach Historical Archive.*

done by naturalist artist Louis Fuertes. The total cost of the hotel with all its fittings was estimated at $1.25 million. Room rates, on the American Plan that included meals, were $15 to $20 a day.

The Flamingo got a blast of national publicity a few weeks after its opening when president-elect Warren G. Harding came to Miami and Carl Fisher brought him, unscheduled, to Miami Beach. After lunch at the Lincoln Hotel and a round of golf, Harding stayed in one of the Flamingo cottages.

The Flamingo was a perfect vantage point for the speedboat racing that Carl Fisher had started on a two-mile course he had set up in the bay, from the Flamingo Hotel down to Sixth Street. There were also polo grounds for the Flamingo located south of Lincoln Road between Meridian and Lenox Avenues, with a grandstand at Jefferson Avenue. In fact, the polo field predated the Flamingo Hotel, opening on February 20, 1919. Fisher was a sportsman who took part in both these sports himself. Tea dances after the polo games were part of the social life at the Flamingo.

It was hard to demolish the Flamingo. It had been constructed of poured concrete and steel rods; its tower was out of range of the wrecking ball, and cables couldn't pull it down. The city refused to allow the use of dynamite, so the Flamingo was taken down by jackhammers in 1960.[161]

The Nautilus Hotel

The Nautilus was probably Fisher's best hotel. The architects, Leonard Schultze and engineer S. Fullerton Weaver, had just formed a partnership in 1921. Schultze had studied at the École des Beaux-Arts in Paris. Prior to the Nautilus, Schultze & Weaver designed the Los Angeles Biltmore, and afterward they would create the Coral Gables Biltmore, the Roney Plaza in Miami Beach, the Sherry-Netherland and Waldorf-Astoria Hotels in New York and many others. In 1926, they designed Montauk Manor for Carl Fisher in his next development venture, Montauk, Long Island.

The Nautilus opened on January 10, 1924, on the bay at Forty-third Street. Of six stories, with twin domed towers reaching higher, it had 183 rooms and villas at a total cost, including landscaping and furnishings, of $1.25 million.[162] It had an X-shaped floor plan, with all rooms commanding a view. The style was elegant Spanish Colonial:

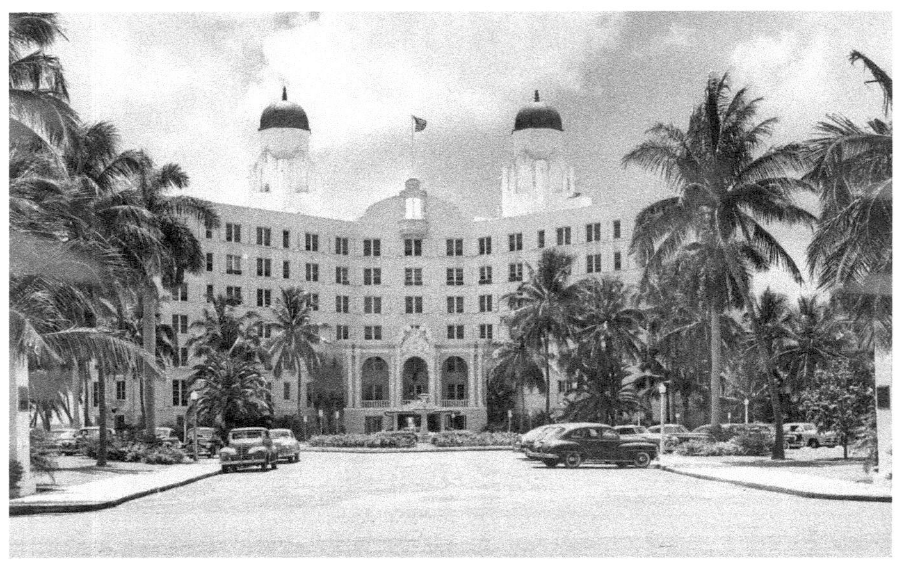

The Nautilus Hotel, on Biscayne Bay at Forty-third Street, was designed by Schultze & Weaver. *Courtesy City of Miami Beach Historical Archive.*

> *The Nautilus, built in 1924, was one of Carl Fisher's most luxurious hotels. The baroque entrance, curved parapets, and the twin church-like towers were among the Spanish decorative elements employed by the architectural firm of Schultze and Weaver in their first commission in the Miami area.*[163]

Fisher had pumped up two small islands, Johns and Collins Islands, just offshore from the Nautilus that were also used by guests. Johns Island had a dance floor and teahouse; the larger Collins Island had sixteen furnished rental villas and the broadcast tower for radio station WIOD (Wonderful Isle of Dreams). In a newspaper ad placed by the Nautilus, Schultze & Weaver are credited with designing the "hotel proper," but Kiehnel & Elliott, whom we have met before, were the architects for the "dormitory, tea house, and cottages."[164]

During World War II, the Nautilus served as a military hospital, and it never returned to hotel use. After the war, it was used by the Veterans Administration; then in 1949, the Mount Sinai Hospital of Greater Miami purchased it. (The hospital became Mount Sinai Medical Center in 1971.) Johns and Collins Islands were filled in for parking lots, and the Nautilus building, which had become outmoded as a hospital facility, was torn down in 1968.

FORTY-FIRST STREET

Before constructing the Nautilus, Fisher had prepared the landscape that would surround it, in the vicinity of Forty-first Street. This was originally John Collins's farm road running through his avocado orchards. As Miami Beach developed, the orchards began to be platted as building lots in 1921. A 1923 map shows streets laid out in the First Orchard Subdivision, and just south of the City Limits, the "Bay Shore Dairy Farm" and a "Negro Colony."

Prior to 1920, Fisher had established a dairy near present-day Chase Avenue that supplied milk products for his hotels. In 1922, it had 135 cows.[165] But Fisher had planned to dredge a lake in this area, so in 1923, the dairy was moved to Miami:

> *The pasturage of the dairy was at the point where Surprise Lake was designated. Work had to begin and the Miami Beach dairy as established here came to an end. Already plans have been made to utilize the dairy buildings as polo dormitories…and the cow sheds as polo stables.*[166]

Dredges then carved out Surprise Lake and its three connecting waterways. Four polo fields were laid out on the filled-in land to the west of the Biscayne

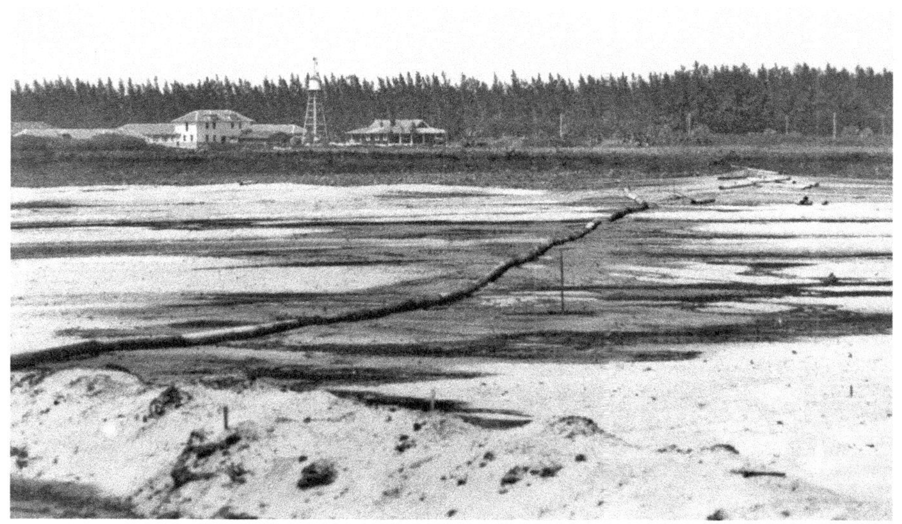

The Miami Beach Dairy, near Chase Avenue and Forty-first Street, in 1920, with "dredge pipes in position for filling the low ground." *Courtesy City of Miami Beach Historical Archive.*

Waterway. Polo games were moved from the Flamingo to the Nautilus grounds in 1925.

It was also in this area that Fisher had planned, in 1919, a $40,000 "industrial colony" for the laborers he employed. It would start with twelve houses, designed by Henry La Pointe, on three acres, in addition to a store, meeting room, church and movie theater. It would be exclusively for blacks.[167] It apparently didn't materialize entirely as planned, but the 1926 city directory lists a "Fisher Colony," with sixteen units, near Forty-second Street and Prairie Avenue. Most of the tenants were carpenters. In 1926, the Miami Beach Bayshore Company, one of Fisher's, built a two-story apartment house at 4220 Prairie Avenue, with twelve units. It cost $50,000 and was called the Fisher Apartments.

Two inhabitants of the "Colony House" in 1924 were Kotaro Suto and Aaron Yarnell. Suto was Carl Fisher's Japanese gardener, whose skill in landscaping transformed Fisher's raw land into a tropical paradise. Suto ran his own plant nursery on Chase Avenue in later years.

Aaron Yarnell (1878–1952), a black man born in Tennessee, was hired as a laborer, but when Fisher acquired an elephant named Carl in 1921 and added Rosie in 1923, Yarnell was found to have a special talent with the animals and became the official elephant trainer. The elephants helped with construction work, gave cart rides for children, caddied for President

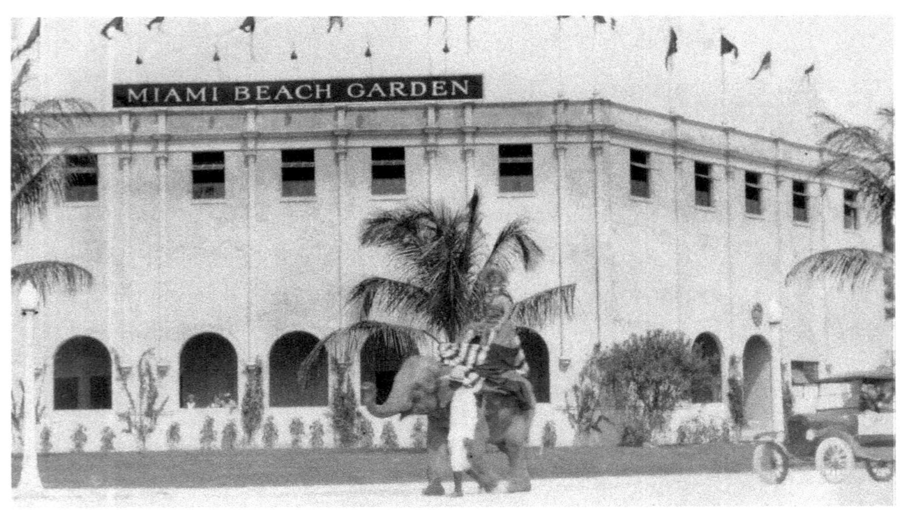

The Miami Beach Garden, with Carl Fisher's elephant, Rosie, led by her trainer Aaron Yarnell. *Courtesy City of Miami Beach Historical Archive.*

Harding's golf game and provided wonderful publicity photos. Aaron Yarnell is seen in the accompanying photo leading Rosie.

In the background of this picture is another lost feature of Forty-first Street: the Miami Beach Garden. This was a large amphitheater in the shape of an elongated octagon that stood on the south side of Forty-first Street between Alton Road and its namesake, Garden Avenue. It is surprising that this building has been so completely forgotten. When Carl Fisher Properties built it in 1924, it was the largest building in the city. Its outer dimensions were 203 feet in length and 145 feet in width, with a seating capacity of four thousand. August Geiger designed it[168] in the Beaux-Arts style. The Garden, it was hoped, "will feature high-class amusements ranging from boxing exhibitions to grand opera...Roller polo and ice skating will be first introduced to Florida here during the winter."[169] The Miami Beach Garden officially opened on January 15, 1924, with roller-polo team practice. In 1926, just a few days before the September hurricane, it was announced that Carl Fisher Properties planned to remodel the Garden "for use as an open-air theatre this winter."[170]

The accompanying photo was taken just after the hurricane, showing the auditorium apparently intact. For those familiar with Saint Patrick's Church, that is not what you see in the distance here—it wasn't built until 1928. This is not a view looking south down Alton Road, but rather it looks west down Forty-first Street, and the buildings in the background include two houses by the bay that Walter DeGarmo designed in 1924 and 1925 for George

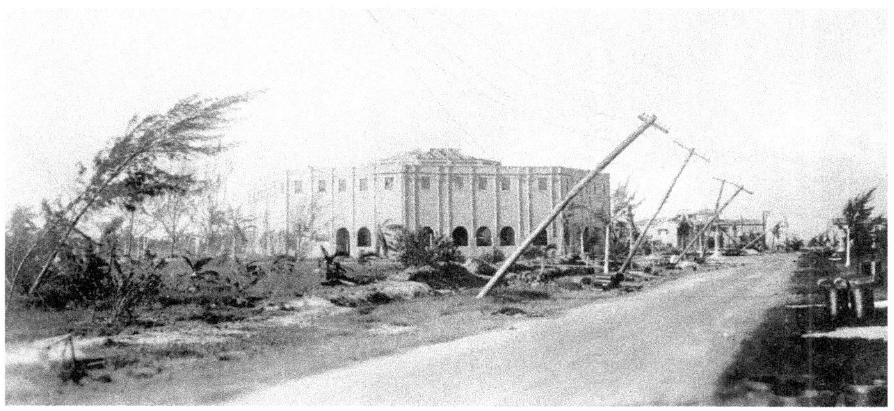

The Garden Auditorium after the 1926 hurricane. This view looks west along Forty-first Street to the bay, where the Julia Tuttle Causeway is now. *Courtesy City of Miami Beach Historical Archive.*

S. Hasbrouck of Berwyn, Pennsylvania. (His wife, Lucille, was the sister of treasury secretary Andrew Mellon.) These homes were demolished in 1958 for the construction of the Julia Tuttle Causeway.

Despite the hurricane, the auditorium remodeling took place as planned "with the installation of a stage, built in New York and shipped here, so that Broadway successes might be staged in the truly metropolitan manner."[171] The Garden Theatre opened on January 16, 1927, with the play *Just Married*, a comedy that had run in New York, Philadelphia, Chicago and Boston. In the 1930s, the Garden lived up to its name as the venue for the annual International Tropical Flower Show. Many local residents, as well as nurseries, put on displays, and dozens of silver trophies were awarded. The building's curving, tiered floor was found to be well suited for this purpose.[172] But the Miami Beach Garden disappears from city directories after 1938.

The King Cole Hotel

Fisher's next hotel, the King Cole, was built in 1925 still farther north, on the south bank of Lake Surprise at Forty-seventh Street. Designed by Kiehnel & Elliott, it was a long, low, three-story building with a square tower at one end, topped with a peaked roof. A distinctive feature was a long, freestanding veranda—with rounded arches, of course—that was set apart from the main building so that gatherings would not disturb the other guests. The hotel was described at its completion:

> *Although small in size as compared with the other Miami Beach hostelries of the Carl G. Fisher properties, it is expected to set a new record in elaborate structure, accommodations and furnishings. Containing only 60 guest rooms, the structure represents an investment of nearly $400,000...Although the general architecture will be Spanish in character, the legend of Old King Cole will predominate throughout. The lounge will be decorated with five large oil paintings...representing the "jolly old soul" in various roles. These paintings are now being completed by the noted artist Howard Hilder. The dining room will have a particularly rustic design with ornamental and heraldic features of the eleventh century.*[173]

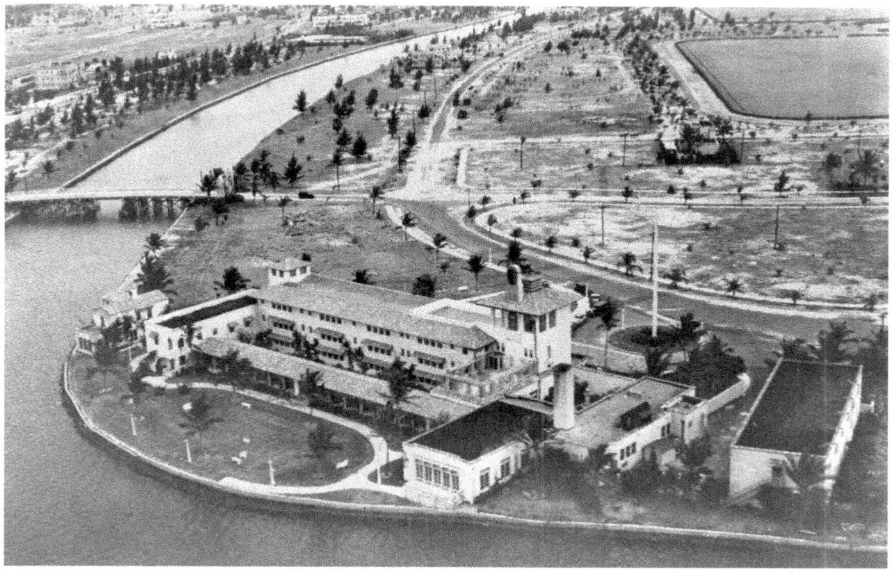

Aerial view of the King Cole Hotel, where the Biscayne Waterway meets Lake Surprise. This view looks south, with the Nautilus polo fields at upper right. *Courtesy Arva Moore Parks.*

Like the Nautilus, the King Cole served as a military hospital during World War II. Later, it housed the Miami Heart Institute, but the original King Cole building was demolished in August 1965.

THE BOULEVARD HOTEL

Carl Fisher's last Miami Beach hotel, the Boulevard, opened in August 1926, a month before the hurricane. The building conformed to the triangular shape of its lot, at the convergence of Dade Boulevard and Meridian Avenue. It stood in the golf course across from the Collins Canal, and its enclosed rooftop terrace had commanding views. The architect was Englishman William F. Brown, who also designed many of the Ocean Beach buildings described in Chapter 2. The Boulevard was less luxurious than Fisher's other hotels and catered to a middle-class clientele; its rates in 1927 (six to seven dollars for a double room) were half that of the Flamingo (twelve to twenty). The Boulevard's cafeteria-style dining room served "plain, American home

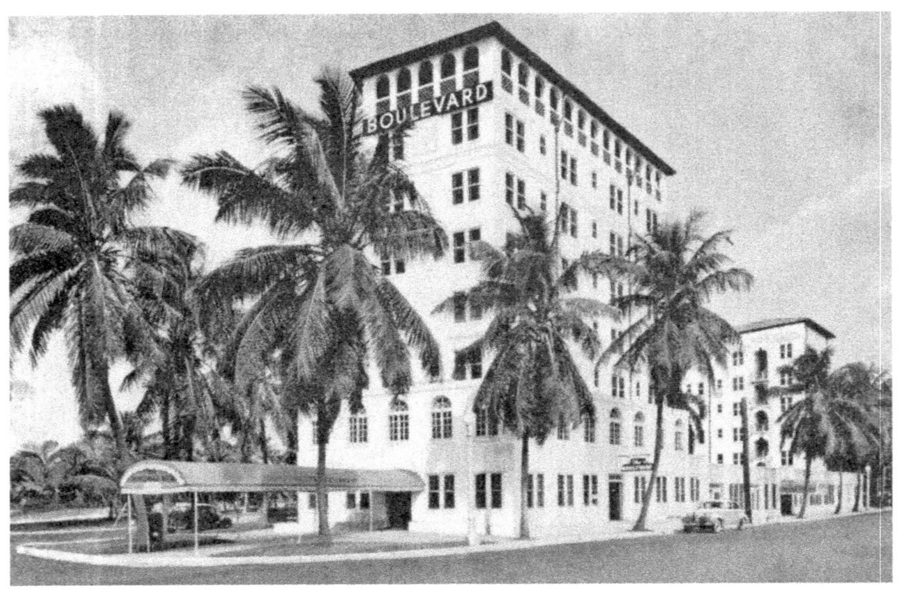

Carl Fisher's fifth Miami Beach hotel was the Boulevard, on the north side of Dade Boulevard at Meridian Avenue. *Postcard courtesy of Larry Wiggins.*

cooking"[174] and was open to the public. Still, the building did have elegant Spanish touches: clay tile on the hip roof and short tower; rounded arches; stone balustrades; and a central terrace. The lobby had ornamental twisted columns, rounded arches and a stone balustrade around the mezzanine.

The Boulevard Hotel, like so many others, served as a barracks in World War II. After the war, it became a retirement hotel and was demolished in 1980, the last of Fisher's hotels to be built and the last to go.

After the Boulevard, Fisher went off to his next big project: developing a summer resort at Montauk, New York, at the eastern tip of Long Island. There, he had his Nautilus architects Schultze & Weaver design a Tudor-style lodge, the Montauk Inn, which still stands as the only surviving Carl Fisher hotel.

CHAPTER 10

OTHER HOTELS

Carl Fisher's Flamingo Hotel, on the bay at Fifteenth Street, was the city's first grand hotel. Others were soon to follow. Two of them, the Fleetwood and the Floridian, together with the Flamingo, were the "three F's" along the bay front.

FLEETWOOD HOTEL

Retired realtor J. Perry Stoltz from New York and Ohio built the Fleetwood, named for his son, after coming to Miami Beach on vacation in 1923 and getting caught up in the Florida boom. The building permit was issued in May 1924, and the towering Fleetwood, the tallest hotel in Florida at the time, opened on January 15, 1925. It had five hundred feet of waterfront on the bay at Eighth Street. With furnishings, it had cost $2 million. A signed rendering identifies the architect as Frank V. Newell,[175] who had designed the 1902 Windsor Hotel in Jacksonville, Florida, after an earlier Windsor burned. The Fleetwood was austere and rectilinear, with none of the Mediterranean flourishes. It had nine-story wings on the north and south and a fifteen-story center section. Projecting horizontal ridges foreshadow (no pun intended) the "eyebrows" of later Art Deco buildings. The Fleetwood was open year-round and had 350 guest rooms, and in 1928, the daily rate for a double room was twelve to eighteen dollars. The ninth floor, at the top of the side

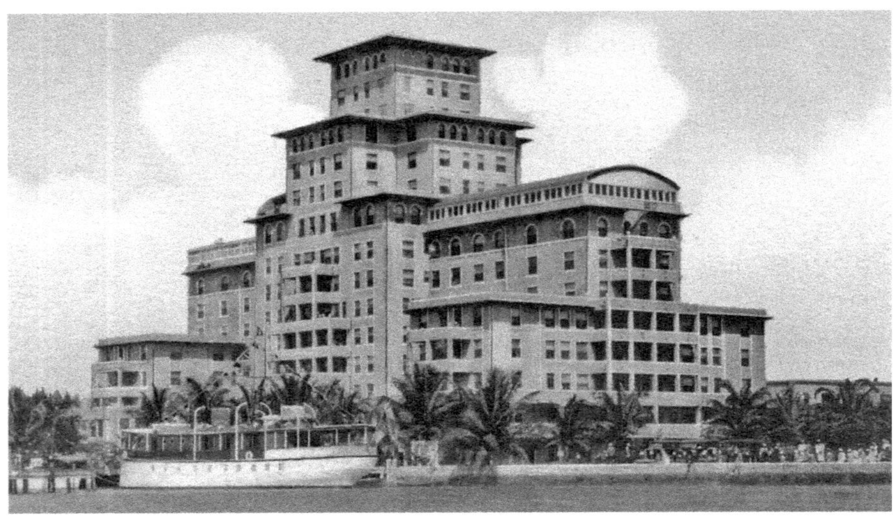

The Fleetwood Hotel, viewed from Biscayne Bay, opened in 1925. A few years later, an enclosed dining room was put on the roof of the south wing, seen at right. *Postcard courtesy of Larry Wiggins.*

wings, had entertainment facilities: the Palm Room, ballroom and roof garden. There was dining and dancing Monday through Saturday to a live orchestra. The Fleetwood also broadcast radio station WMBF, "Wonderful Miami Beach Florida," and served as a barracks for military recruits during World War II. It was demolished in 1966.

Floridian Hotel

Jerome Cherbino (originally Cherbineau) had worked at a cattle ranch in southwest Texas before coming to Miami in 1919 and going into real estate.[176] In January 1925, he bought James Allison's aquarium at the end of the County Causeway for $500,000, demolished it and in July started construction of the Floridian, on the bay between Fifth and Sixth Streets. Its architect was Samuel D. Butterworth (1869–1935) from Lansing, Michigan, who also had a home in Miami Beach. Ten stories high and with 242 rooms, the Floridian opened in January 1926. The building had a few Spanish touches—a tile-roofed tower and cast-stone embellishments at the roofline—but the lobby was most outstanding, with the domed ceiling of a rotunda decorated with murals.

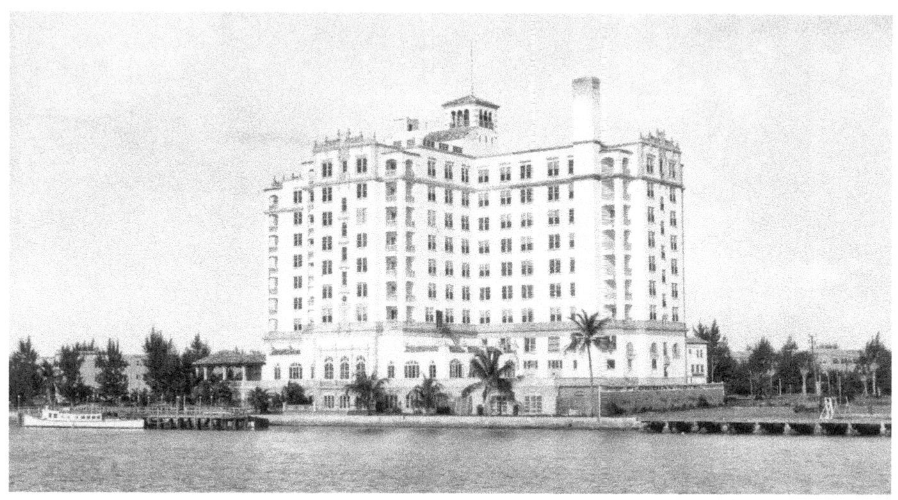

The Floridian Hotel was built in 1925 on the former site of the Aquarium. *Postcard courtesy of Larry Wiggins.*

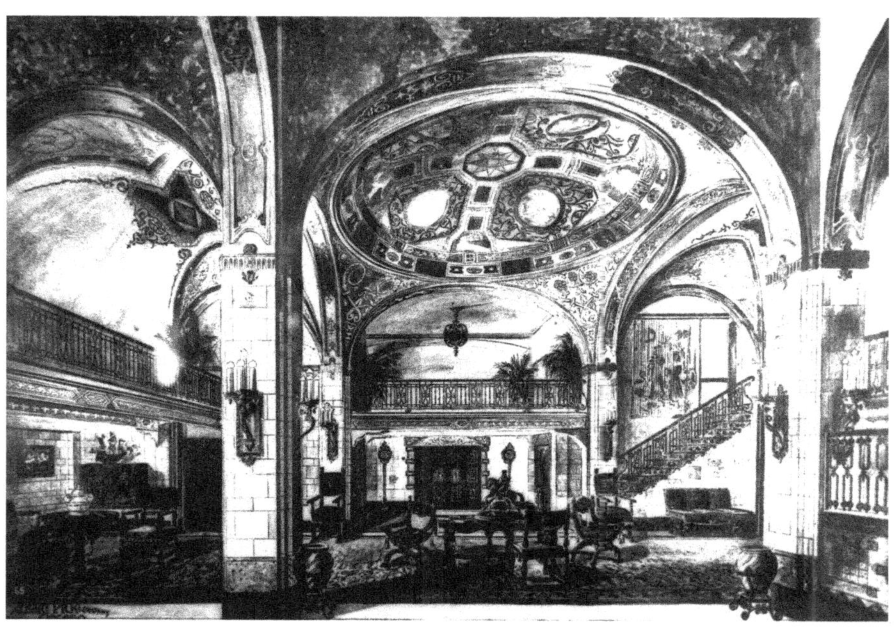

The Floridian Hotel lobby with its ornate domed ceiling, in a rendering by the Albert Pick Hotel Company of Chicago. *Courtesy Miami-Dade Public Library, Gleason Romer archive F00851.*

The Floridian had a supper club with top-name entertainment and was notorious for its penthouse gambling casino. Al Capone was said to have a quarter interest in it. W.C. Fields stayed at the hotel in March 1929. During World War II, like so many other Miami Beach hotels, the Floridian also served as a barracks. After the war, it became a retirement home and in 1959 went into foreclosure. The building was quite run down, but the interior was mostly intact. Its new owner renamed it the Biscaya and fought to save it, but it became such an eyesore at the entrance to the city that those who wanted it gone prevailed, and it was dynamited in 1987.[177]

DEAUVILLE HOTEL

Joseph Elsener, from New York, came to Miami Beach around 1923 and became one of Carl Fisher's top salesmen. In August 1925, he got a building permit for the Deauville Casino, an entertainment center that also had hotel rooms, on the ocean at Sixty-seventh Street. It opened in January 1926 as a lavish gambling casino and beach club, although Elsener himself never gambled. The Deauville also had the largest swimming pool in Florida, filled with saltwater, where celebrity Johnny Weismuller performed. As Howard Kleinberg describes it:

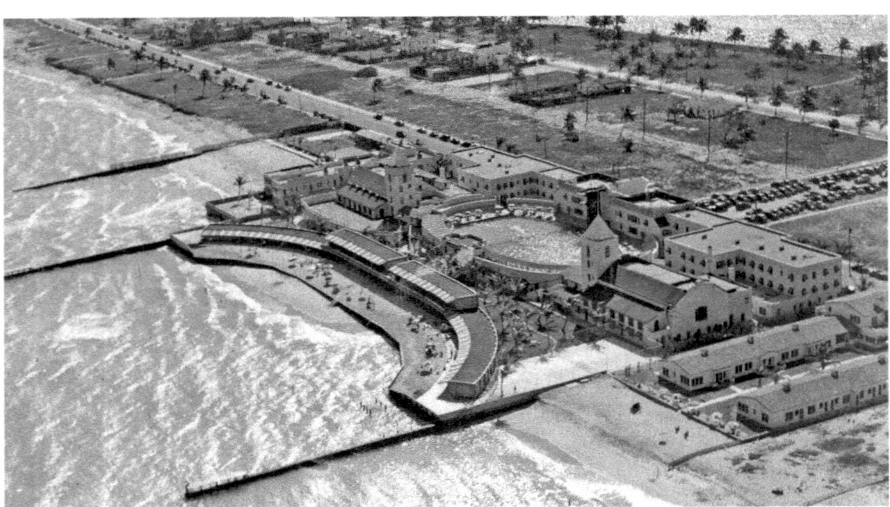

Aerial view of the Deauville Hotel with its huge swimming pool, built in 1925. Indian Creek is at the top. *Postcard courtesy of Larry Wiggins.*

The pool was 165 feet long and 100 feet wide and located on the second floor behind the hotel rooms. Planned as an entertainment capital, the Deauville provided dining rooms, ballroom dancing, entertainers, exhibitions by champion swimmers and divers and state-of-the-art bathing facilities.[178]

It was a wonderful place, but its location was too far north of town, and the September 1926 hurricane dealt it heavy damage. In 1928, it was in receivership and was sold at public auction. The new owner, the Deauville Casino Corporation, kept Joseph Elsener on as general manager.[179] It was sold again, for $200,000, in 1934 and, in 1936, was leased to health guru and publisher Bernarr Macfadden, who ran it as a sort of health spa called the Macfadden Deauville. In December 1956, as the Deauville was being demolished "to make way for a new hotel and shopping center,"[180] an acetylene torch caught the debris on fire and finished the process. Architect Melvin Grossman designed a new Deauville Hotel in its place.

Pancoast Hotel

As we have seen, Carl Fisher sold his oceanfront land for private estates, and he put his hotels elsewhere. The first grand oceanfront hotel in Miami Beach, even before the Deauville, was the Pancoast, constructed at Twenty-ninth Street in 1923. Architects were Martin L. Hampton and Emil A. Ehmann, who had formed a partnership that year. Ehmann had previously worked in Jacksonville and for a time had been Florida's supervising architect for public buildings.[181] In July 1923, Hampton had gone on a sketching trip to Spain for firsthand study of Mediterranean architecture.[182]

The Pancoast was the project of John Collins's grandson J. Arthur Pancoast. The building permit was issued on May 31, 1923, for this $248,000 top-class hotel with 161 rooms, and it opened in January 1924. The Pancoast had the sprawling, multi-level layout of the Mediterranean style, with multiple hip and gable roofs of clay tile.

Like some Spanish castle, with its courts, arches, mazes of color, window balconies, tower and promenade verandahs, the Pancoast, modernized to the nth degree, stands out as the very incarnation of antiquity...Mr. Hampton spent months in various parts of Spain, diligently studying the kind of architecture appropriate for the Pancoast...No details of Spanish design

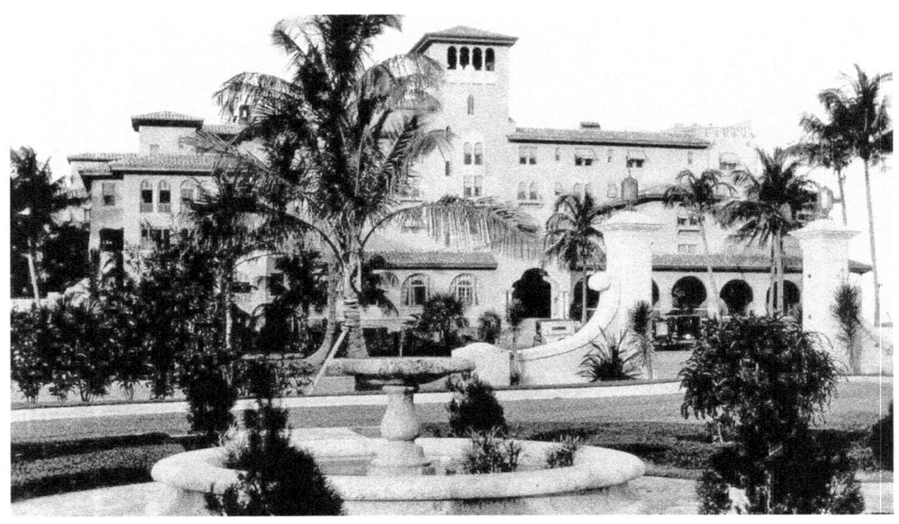

John Collins's grandson J. Arthur Pancoast opened the Pancoast Hotel in 1923, on the ocean at Twenty-ninth Street. *Postcard courtesy of Larry Wiggins.*

> *have been overlooked, yet no modern conveniences have been sacrificed to carry out the exact style.*[183]

There were four to five stories to the main part of the building, and an "Old Spanish Watchtower"[184] that rose to seven. The building faced south onto a circular drive that had a park with a fountain in the center. In addition, an auxiliary three-story building called The Lodge, somewhat more modest but still with a tower and arcade, stood half a block to the west, down Twenty-ninth Street. This may have been the promised accommodations for guests' chauffeurs and servants.

During World War II, the Pancoast served as a military hospital. It was demolished in 1955 and replaced by Melvin Grossman's Seville Hotel. There are many other lost works of Martin Hampton, but the Pancoast was one of his finest.

Lost Works of Martin L. Hampton

Martin Luther Hampton (1891–1950)[185] was from South Carolina and went to Columbia University in New York. He came to Miami in 1914 and

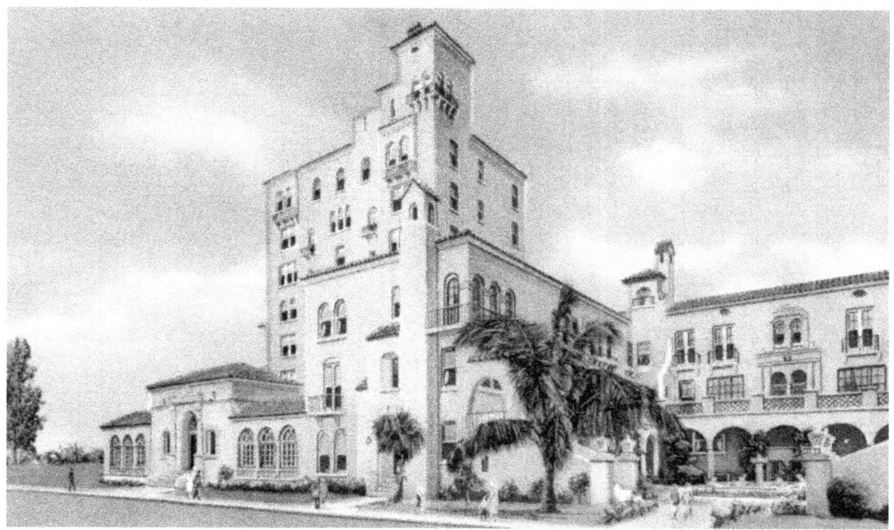

Martin L. Hampton designed the Helene Apartments in 1921 and the adjoining Helene Hotel, completed three years later. Its eight-story tower was a landmark on Fifteenth Street between Michigan and Lenox Avenues. *Postcard courtesy of Larry Wiggins.*

returned there after serving overseas in World War I. A rendering of the Roman Pools on Twenty-third Street in Miami Beach, signed "M. Luther Hampton 1917,"[186] indicates that, as one of his first projects, he remodeled the earlier bathhouse there for Carl Fisher.

In 1921, Hampton and H. George Fink went to work on George Merrick's Coral Gables development as its first two architects, but Hampton continued to design in Miami Beach, Miami, and Palm Beach as well. In 1922, Hampton remodeled Fink's 1919 BAY SHORE GOLF CLUBHOUSE in Miami Beach, enlarging it and adding two domes to the roof. This clubhouse was demolished in 1954.

Another project of Hampton's in Miami Beach was the Helene, built by Eugene C. Stahl on the south side of Fifteenth Street between Michigan and Lenox Avenues. It started as the three-story HELENE APARTMENTS, built in 1921 at the west end of the block. It was classic Mediterranean style, with a central courtyard, rounded arches, stone columns and two grand exterior stairs. In 1924, Stahl added the HELENE HOTEL to its east, joining the two with a series of arches. (The hotel foundations were laid in 1922, but construction had been "held up.")[187] The hotel was a seven-story tower, plus an enclosure for a water tank on the roof to provide enough water pressure for its height. Its style was described as "Spanish-Moorish type."[188] The hotel lobby was in a separate structure in front, and the dining room was on the ground floor, overlooking the golf course to the south. The Helene tower was a prominent landmark, only a few blocks east of the Flamingo Hotel. Martin Hampton designed both parts of the Helene. The apartments were demolished as an unsafe structure in 1973 and the tower in 1974. The vacant lots became an employee parking lot for the telephone company across the street.

In 1922, Hampton designed the magnificent Community Theatre on Lincoln Road, completed in 1923, which is described in Chapter 8. In 1925, Hampton & Ehmann designed the Gulfstream Apartments, on the ocean at Sixtieth Street, which is described and pictured in Chapter 6. Hampton's five-story Good Hotel, named for owner Chester A. Good, followed in 1933. Situated on the ocean at Forty-third Street and facing south, the Good is often mistaken for the earlier Pancoast Hotel. Both were in the Mediterranean style, but the Good had three towers while the Pancoast had one. The Good Hotel was torn down in 1976. Martin Hampton was also accomplished in the Art Deco style: his streamlined Sheridan Theatre was built in 1937 on Forty-first Street at Sheridan Avenue. A five-story office building replaced it in 1985.

Lest this should get too depressing, some of Hampton's buildings that still survive are the Mayflower Hotel at 1700 Alton Road (1922), Hampton Court Apartments at 2800 Collins Avenue (1924), the Hampton Hotel at 940 Lincoln Road (1926) and Old City Hall on Washington Avenue (1927).

Roney Plaza Hotel

We have seen many other projects by Newton B.T. Roney around Miami Beach, but in 1925, his crowning achievement was the palatial Roney Plaza Hotel, occupying the entire block on the ocean between Twenty-third and Twenty-fourth Streets, across from the Roman Pools and a few blocks south of the Pancoast. It was designed by the renowned firm of Schultze & Weaver, who had just designed Fisher's Nautilus hotel, as well as the Biltmore Hotel in Coral Gables. Roney's architect, Robert A. Taylor, was the firm's associate in designing the Roney Plaza. With nearly three hundred rooms, it opened in February 1926, at a cost of $1 million, and was called the greatest oceanfront hotel south of Atlantic City, New Jersey.[189] Its floor plan was L-shaped, and it was only nine stories high, but its landmark Spanish Baroque tower at the corner gave it an imposing presence. Schultze & Weaver had put similar

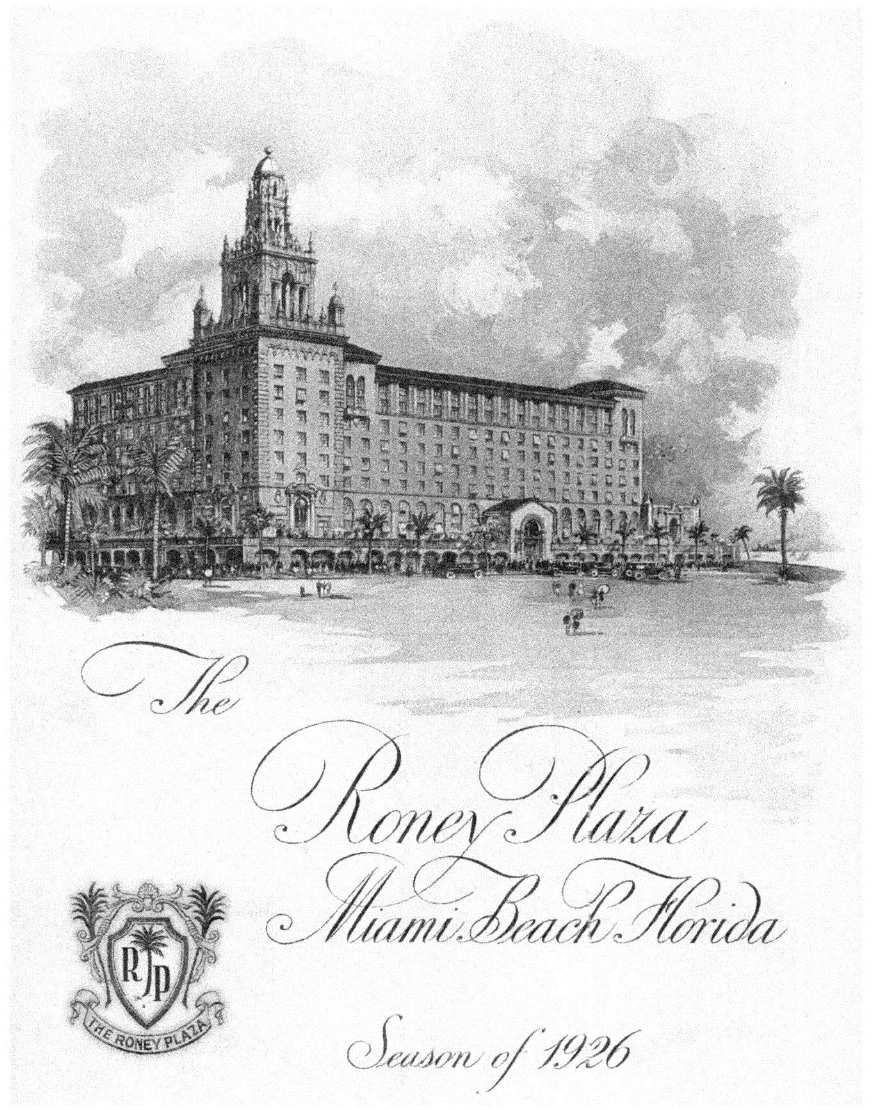

Menu cover from the Roney Plaza Hotel, 1926. *Courtesy City of Miami Beach Historical Archive.*

towers on their Coral Gables Biltmore Hotel and on the Daily News Tower (Freedom Tower), which they designed for James Cox's newspaper in Miami.

The entrance to the Roney Plaza was on the south, and its entire ground floor was devoted to luxury shops. The extensive grounds it enclosed were made into a tropical garden, where tea dances were held three days a week. A $150,000 project in 1930 added more stores, a swimming pool and cabanas; each cabana had a dressing room, shower and shady veranda.

For years, the "Roney" was a popular gathering place for local residents, as well as tourists, but when it reached the age of forty, it was worn and dated but not old enough to be quaint. Unable to compete with the new resorts, it closed in May 1968 and was demolished on August 1.

In the 1920s, the Roney Plaza and Pancoast Hotels were connected by a promenade that was the fashionable place to be. In the days before the crash, the well-heeled guests at the Pancoast and the Roney Plaza could stroll along the Promenade to check on their investments on the big board. Just south of the Pancoast Hotel was the beautiful Beaux-Arts oceanfront office of Thomson McKinnon stockbrokers, built in the summer of 1929 and designed by L.M. Barrett. A few blocks farther south, at 2629 Collins Avenue, was another brokerage: the office for Harris Upham and Company. Palm Beach architect Addison Mizner designed it, his only known building in Miami Beach, in 1928. Mizner was remodeling the Palm Beach mansion of stockbroker John F. Harris that same year. This office was rather plain on the outside, but according to Mizner expert Donald Curl:

> *It had an impressive 48- by 32-foot brokerage room with 15-foot ceilings and a large working fireplace. A center hall separated the brokerage room from two ornate offices and a secretary's room. On the second floor Mizner designed a pied-a-terre for Harris of two master bedrooms, a servant's room, and a small kitchen.*[190]

Speaking of the crash, we now come to one of the great Depression-era architects of Miami Beach.

LOST WORKS OF ROY F. FRANCE

Roy Franklin France (1888–1972), a native of Minnesota, was educated at the Chicago Armour Institute and the Chicago Technical School, and he started his architectural career in Chicago. His early buildings there have been documented by the Commission on Chicago Historical and Architectural Landmarks. They include a Gothic-style garage and a half dozen apartment buildings in the Tudor, Classical and Craftsman styles, built of brick and stone, dating from 1913 to 1928.

France's sojourn in South Florida began with William F. Whitman, the Chicago publisher who built a house on Miami Beach in 1918. As noted in Chapter 7, his son Stanley is the source of much information. His father brought France to Miami Beach as the architect for a planned hotel, but France first designed an apartment building for Whitman in 1931: the Indian Creek Apartments, at 3300 Collins Avenue. It was a sturdy, three-story Mediterranean-style building with round-arched doors and windows, stone balustrades, a barrel-tile roof and a rooftop tower. It was demolished in 1966. The building contractor for the Indian Creek was D. Richard (Dick) Mead (1899–1993), a prominent community leader who plays a further role in this story.

Originally from Illinois, the Mead family came to Miami Beach and, in 1922, formed the Mead Brothers Construction Company, which did early work for Carl Fisher. They built their own Mead Building in 1928 at 901 Lincoln Road, on the former site of the Eunice Martin School. Dick Mead served on the city council from 1926 to 1934 and started a mortgage and insurance firm in 1938. He strongly promoted Lincoln Road, succeeding August Geiger as president of the Lincoln Road Association in 1938.[191]

In the meantime, the Depression had set in. Newton Roney had taken over Whitman's project on Espanola Way but couldn't keep up the mortgage. As Stanley Whitman recalls, "Everyone was strapped. Roney couldn't pay for the land, and gave the Matanzas [Hotel] to my father in exchange." Since construction was in a slump, there was no work for an architect, so Whitman gave France the job of managing the Matanzas Hotel on Espanola Way.

At one point, Stanley relates, Roney took Whitman up to the tower of the Roney Plaza Hotel and got Whitman to lend him $250,000 on a third mortgage—comparable to $3.5 million in 2014. "Things happened back then that just don't happen today," Stanley muses. Without the loan, Roney would have lost the Roney Plaza to his creditors. The money enabled him to add cabanas, a dance patio and tennis courts to the hotel and helped it recover.

In 1935, Whitman brought his plans for a hotel to fruition and had Roy France design the Whitman Hotel at 3315 Collins Avenue, on the ocean just north of Whitman's home. By then, the tropical surroundings had changed France's design style forever. The Whitman was a classic example of Moderne, or Art Deco style, and the first of several France hotels that came to define the skyline in this part of the beach in the 1930s. The Whitman had a domed tower that soared above the hotel's ten stories, and the front

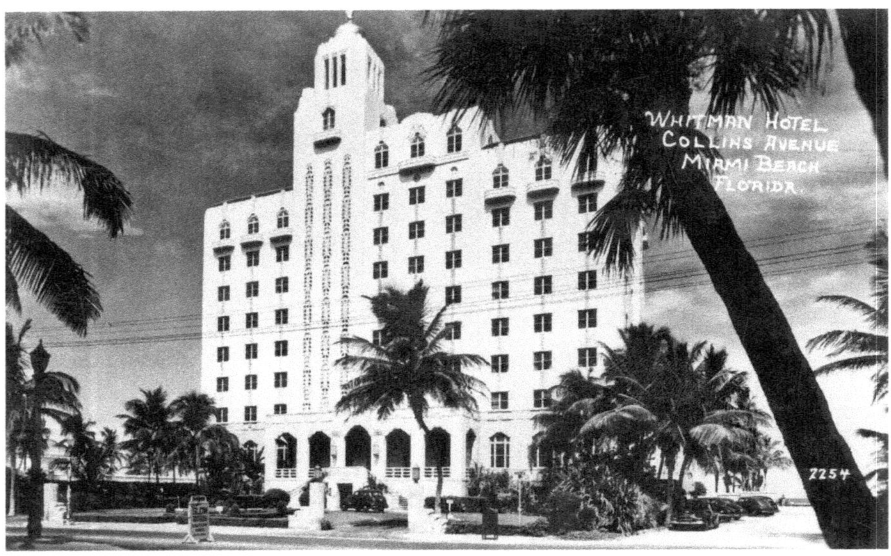

Roy F. France designed the Whitman Hotel for William Whitman in 1935. It stood on Collins Avenue at Thirty-third Street and was later renamed the Robert Richter. *Postcard courtesy of Larry Wiggins.*

was embellished with lacy stone bas-reliefs. The building cost $250,000, but the furnishings doubled that—this during the Depression.

Jeweler Joseph Richter bought the Whitman Hotel in about 1946, making it the first hotel in Miami Beach to sell for $1 million. Richter renamed it for his son, Robert Richter, who had been killed in the war. In 1963, a new owner, Morris Lansburgh, demolished it. Lansburgh had also bought the Saxony Hotel next door, which France had designed in 1948 on the former site of the Whitman home, and Lansburgh wanted to provide more open space for the Saxony guests.[192]

In 1936, Roy France went to work for the Meads and designed the $125,000, six-story SHOREMEDE HOTEL to the north of the Whitman. The Meads had traded William Whitman some of their Lincoln Road property in exchange for the land. The Shoremede had more Mediterranean references than did the Whitman, with multiple gable and hip roofs in clay barrel-tile.

In 1936, France also designed the six-story BRAZNELL HOTEL at 4300 Collins Avenue. (It was next to the earlier, three-story Braznell Apartments, designed by A. Ten Eyck Brown in 1925. That same year, Brown, from Atlanta, and August Geiger designed the Dade County Courthouse in Miami.) The Braznell Hotel had a tower, as many of France's hotels did, and round-arched windows, small balconies and a clay tile roof. In later years, it was called the International Hotel, demolished in 1996. The Braznell Apartments had gone in 1961.

The BELMAR HOTEL was built in 1937, on the ocean on the north side of Twenty-sixth Street. It was an eight-story Art Deco–style building with

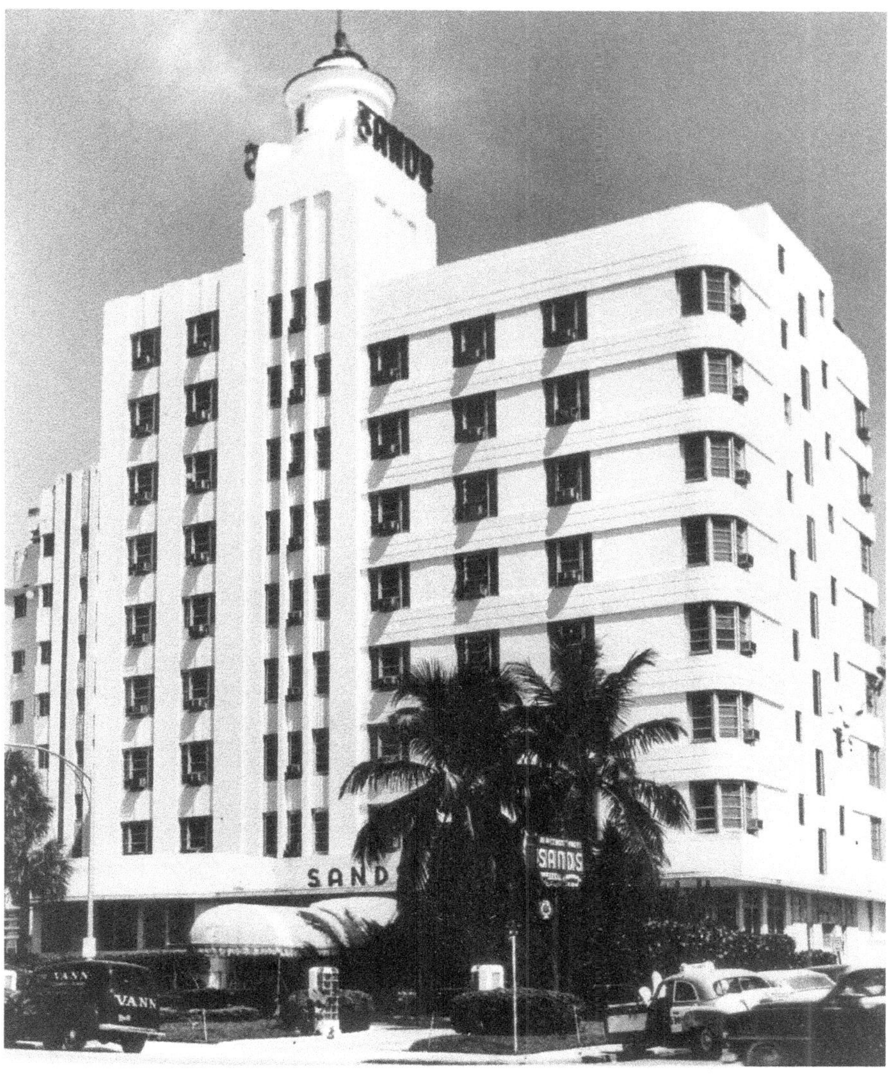

On the ocean at Sixteenth Street, Roy France's Sands Hotel was demolished in 1992. Henry Hohauser's New Yorker Hotel next door to it (far left) went down in April 1981. *Courtesy Arva Moore Parks.*

square columns supporting an eyebrow, or horizontal ridge, over the front terrace. Ribbed vertical panels on the front and sides gave it lift. The seventy-six-room Belmar cost $350,000 furnished. In 1939, France designed a fifty-seven-room addition.

Inside, the lounge had a richly patterned terrazzo floor and a keyhole doorway, and there was a card room on the mezzanine. Hotels served a different function for tourists in the 1930s than they do today. With no air conditioning or in-room entertainment other than radio, the room was just a place to sleep and change clothes. Guests spent most of their time outdoors, at sports or on the beach, and the hotel lobby was the place to socialize. Hotel dining rooms and, after Prohibition, cocktail lounges figured prominently as well.

Other hotels, now lost, that Roy France designed in 1939 included the WHITE HOUSE and JEFFERSON at Fifteenth Street and Ocean Drive and, just north of them, the nine-story SANDS HOTEL at 1601 Collins Avenue. An Art Deco landmark with its cylindrical rooftop tower, the Sands had one hundred rooms and cost $170,000. A swimming pool was added in 1940.

Farther north, another work of France in 1939 was the OCEAN GRANDE HOTEL, on the ocean at Thirty-seventh Street. This seven-story structure had a classically symmetrical Art Deco front façade, with two ribbed vertical panels and two rows of decorative roundels. In recent years, the Ocean Grande stood vacant. Although it was in a historic district of the city, it was judged to be in unsafe condition and demolished in 2014.

Roy France designed dozens of other buildings around Miami Beach that are still standing, but our purpose here is to document the lost. After the war, construction resumed, Miami Beach enjoyed a second boom and architectural styles evolved with the times. Most new hotels were built progressively northward. In 1946, Roy France designed the MARTINIQUE HOTEL on Collins Avenue near Sixty-fourth Street. While many existing hotels had been retrofitted with air conditioning by then, the Martinique was the first hotel in Miami Beach to be built with it. The twelve-story Martinique was demolished in 1973.

Building records have been lost for the MONTE CARLO HOTEL, at 6541 Collins Avenue, but other sources confirm that France designed it[193] in 1948. Its style was Postwar Modern, with typical asymmetry. Originally, it had eyebrows—those horizontal ridges above the windows—that wrapped around the southwest corner of the building, and the lobby at this corner had a grid of nine plate-glass windows. This shows how France's design style had changed since his heavy Tudor and Gothic buildings in Chicago. His philosophy of architecture now was: "Let in the air and sun. That's what people come to Florida for."[194]

In 1951, architects Albert Anis and his nephew Melvin Grossman designed an addition to the south side of the Monte Carlo that removed these features. After basement flooding weakened the building's foundations, it was demolished in 2006.

For years, Roy France worked in partnership with his son, Roy F. France Jr. (1912–1957). Roy France Sr. retired in 1969 at age eighty and lived another three years.

Epilogue: The Preservation Movement

It was the hotel buildings that inspired the historic preservation movement in Miami Beach rather than the sumptuous private estates or the civic buildings or theaters, some of which were equally grand.

By 1976, the south end of the city was run-down and crime-ridden, but Miami resident Barbara Capitman, who had long enjoyed South Beach vacations, and her friend artist Leonard Horowitz remembered better times and saw the architectural beauty of the Depression-era hotels along Ocean Drive. Like Collins and Fisher long before, they had a vision of what could be: the hotels fixed up and prosperous again rather than the scorched-earth approach of planned "redevelopment." Capitman, her son Andrew, Horowitz and a small group of other local residents started the Miami Design Preservation League to bring attention to the neighborhood and to prevent its loss.

Through Capitman's persistence, in 1979, the National Register of Historic Places, administered by the U.S. Department of the Interior, designated a one-square-mile area of South Beach as the Miami Beach Architectural Historic District, the second historic district on the register to date from the twentieth century. (The first, in 1975, was Frank Lloyd Wright's campus for Florida Southern College in Lakeland.) Pioneer investors, especially Tony Goldman and Gerry Sanchez, helped the preservationist cause immensely by buying and restoring a number of hotels in the district and demonstrating that preservation was good business. These old buildings, made over into boutique hotels, gave the neighborhood a unique charm, drew tourists and made money.

National Register designation, however, is an honorific title that encourages preservation but does not prevent historic structures from being torn down. That requires local governments to pass their own ordinances;

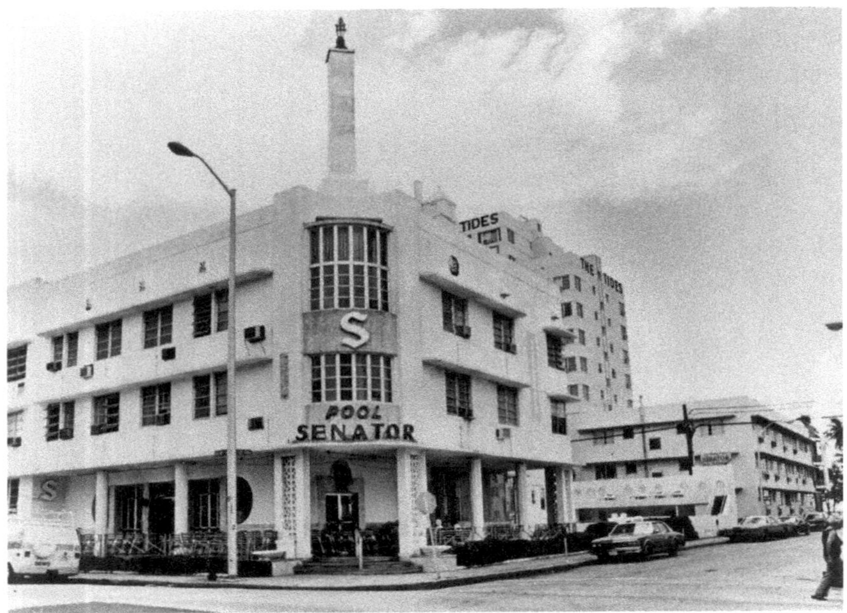

The Senator Hotel shortly before its demolition. This was the state of many South Beach hotels when the preservation movement was getting underway. It took vision to see its original beauty. *Courtesy Arva Moore Parks.*

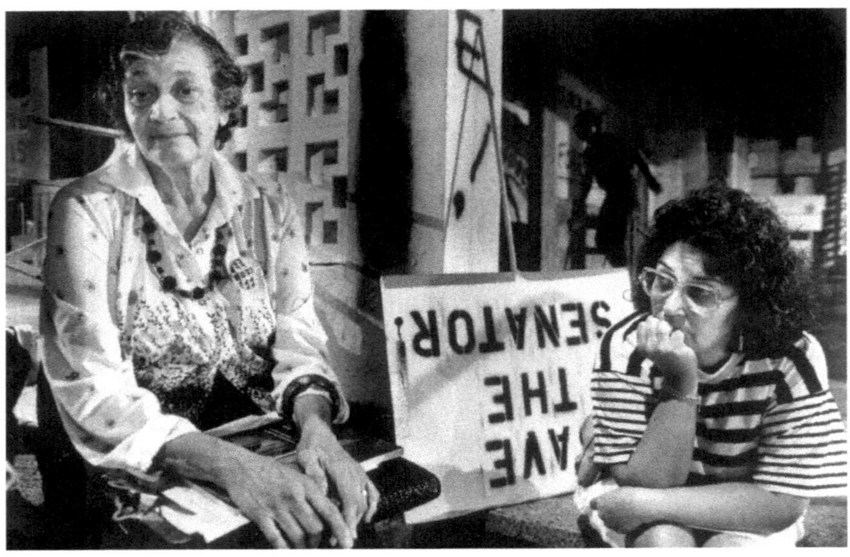

Pioneer preservationists Barbara Capitman (left) and Matti Bower staged a sit-in to prevent the loss of the Senator in 1988. Years later, Ms. Bower became the city's first Hispanic and first female mayor. *Courtesy Arva Moore Parks.*

Miami Beach had none until 1982 and did not designate the Ocean Drive district until 1986. Even then, the rulings were not retroactive, and buildings already slated for demolition were still lost.

Several Art Deco hotels in South Beach, like the old Penn Station in New York City, were martyrs to the cause, their demolition inspiring an appreciation for what was still left. One of the first was the New Yorker at 1611 Collins Avenue, designed by renowned Art Deco architect Henry Hohauser in 1940. Its classic Streamline design stood seven stories high, with an eyebrow arcing around its parapet. It had harbored military trainees in World War II. Its demolition in April 1981 was especially bitter because its owner broke his promise to spare it.[195]

As mentioned above, the 1925 Floridian Hotel, renamed the Biscaya, was destroyed in March 1987 against its owner's wishes because it was judged to be a blight on the city. It was the last of the grand hotels of the 1920s on Miami Beach.

The Senator Hotel, at 1201 Collins Avenue, brought on what Barbara Capitman regarded as a watershed battle.[196] It was designed in 1939 by L. Murray Dixon, one of Miami Beach's most prolific architects. Its lobby had etched-glass windows, and its rooftop signage pylon was a local landmark. Its owners in 1988 argued that they needed the lot for a parking garage for their other hotels. Capitman and other activists camped out on the front steps to ward off the bulldozers, but to no avail. The Senator was torn down in May 1988, but even after many years, the garage was not built.

The Sands Hotel, designed by Roy France in 1939 and mentioned above, was another sad loss in 1992. The New Yorker Hotel next door was already gone, and the Sands site contributed more space for the construction of the Loews Convention Center Hotel a few years later.

But the lost battles should not detract from the amazing success of historic preservation in Miami Beach. The city now has three additional historic districts that are on the National Register and twelve districts, from Ocean Beach to Altos del Mar, that were designated by the city. Two of these local districts are in residential neighborhoods and were initiated by the residents themselves. The architectural styles celebrated in these districts now include MiMo, or Miami Modern, dating from the 1950s and 1960s and seen in some of the apartment towers that replaced Millionaires' Row, and in the Fontainebleau Hotel, which is now a historic site on the National Register.

Miami Beach keeps reinventing itself. Over the course of its first century, many buildings have been lost—whether to storms, neglect or in the name of progress. Land values always seem to trump sentiment. Zoning decisions by city leaders have far-reaching effects. Looking at what has been lost, besides teaching us about the past, inspires us to appreciate what is still around us, discern what is most important and strive to preserve it.

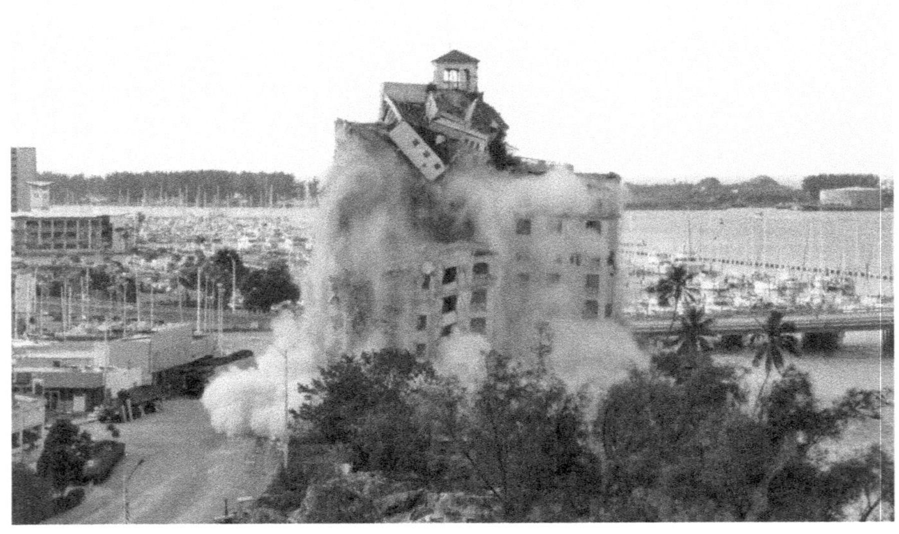

The Floridian Hotel, renamed the Biscaya, was dynamited on Sunday morning, March 15, 1987. *Photograph by the late Charles Buckles, courtesy of James Murphy.*

NOTES

CHAPTER 1

1. Pierce, *Pioneer Life*, 66.
2. *Miami Herald*, "Lifeguard Service Requires Vigilance and Bravery," November 26, 1922, 1-B.
3. Ralph C. Shanks, *U.S. Lifesaving Service: Heroes, Rescues, and Architecture of the Early Coast Guard* (Petaluma, CA: Costano Books, 1996).
4. Pierce, *Pioneer Life*, 70–71.
5. Ibid., 171.
6. Hollingsworth, *History of Dade County*.
7. Lavender, *Miami Beach*, 145.
8. *Miami Herald*, "Old Timer Recalls a Hurricane and a Hanging in South Florida," May 30, 1954, 6-F.
9. *Florida: The East Coast*, 111–13.
10. U.S. Coast Guard Correspondence, 1910–1935, Box 640, National Archives, Washington, D.C.
11. Stuart McIver, *Glimpses of South Florida History* (Miami: Florida Flair Books, 1988), 93.

CHAPTER 2

12. *Miami Herald*, "Miami Beach History Related by Pioneer," November 25, 1926, 16, 18.

13. *Miami Beach Sun*, "Street Names Steeped in Lore and Tradition," March 29, 1959.
14. Kleinberg, *Miami Beach*, 53–54.
15. *Atlas of Miami Beach to Golden Beach* (Philadelphia: Franklin Survey Co., 1935).
16. *Miami News*, December 3, 1920.
17. *Miami Herald*, Obituary, June 7, 1929, 13.
18. *Miami Herald*, "Beach Developer Rites Set," October 5, 1963, 4D.
19. *Miami Herald*, "Smith Company Has Prospered," November 25, 1926, 16.
20. *Miami Herald*, "Miami Beach History."
21. Ibid.
22. *Miami Herald*, "Theater Designer Leader in Field," November 25, 1926, 14.
23. Ibid., photo caption.
24. *Florida: The East Coast*, 243, 261.
25. *Highlights of Greater Miami* (Miami, FL: Greater Miami Publishing Co., 1944), 29.
26. *Miami Herald*, "William Brown, 66, Dies in Hospital," May 13, 1952.
27. Information provided by Carla Granat.
28. Agnes Ash, "Everybody Gamboled at Cook's Casino," *Miami News*, March 20, 1966.
29. *Miami Herald*, "Beach Hotel Sold," March 9, 1969.
30. Kleinberg, *Miami Beach*, 143.
31. Ibid., 236.

Chapter 3

32. *Miami Herald*, "J.S. Collins Dies at the Age of 90," February 11, 1928, 12.
33. Ibid.
34. Ibid.
35. Ibid.
36. Nash, *Magic of Miami Beach*, 103.
37. Carson, *Forty Years*, 12.
38. *Miami Herald*, "Carl Fisher's Plans for a Beach Windmill," November 26, 1916.
39. City of Miami Beach Historical Archive, #1680-24.
40. *Miami News*, "Brilliant and Fascinating Was the Hanan Ball Last Evening," February 7, 1918.
41. *Dade County Florida Deed Book* 148:458.
42. National Parks Service, "James Allison Mansion," www.nps.gov; Library of Congress Historic American Buildings Survey, www.loc.gov/HABS.
43. "Miami Home of James H. Snowden," *Architecture and Building* (September 1917): 85–86.

44. *Miami Herald*, "Reception and Dance by Mr. and Mrs. Snowden," March 30, 1917, 3.
45. *Miami Daily News*, "Edison Avers Rubber Plants are Advancing," March 28, 1930.
46. Kleinberg, *Woggles and Cheese Holes*, 13.
47. *Miami Daily News*, July 26, 1925.
48. "Explains Adaptation of New Architecture," clipping, H. George Fink Scrapbook, private collection.
49. Redford. *Billion Dollar Sandbar*, 86.
50. *Miami Herald*, "J.S. Collins Dies at the Age of 90."

Chapter 4

51. Nash, *Magic of Miami Beach*, 124–25.
52. Edward Ridolph, *Biscayne Bay Trolleys* (Forty Fort, PA: Harold E. Cox, publisher, 1981).
53. *Miami Herald*, "Miami Ocean View Co. Fifth Street Pioneer," February 2, 1925, 2-C.
54. *Miami Daily News and Metropolis*, October 12, 1925.
55. *Miami Herald*, December 15, 1922.

Chapter 5

56. *Miami Beach Sun*, June 21, 1929.
57. *Miami Herald*, "Villa Venice Season Will Last for a Month," March 3, 1934.
58. *Dade County Florida Plat Book* 5:7.
59. *Miami the Beautiful* (Miami, FL: Foster & Reynolds, ca. 1920).
60. Letter, September 23, 1920, quoted in Kleinberg, *Miami Beach*, 73.
61. E.F. Flannery, "Miami's Scenic Highway, Ocean Drive, Has Charmed Thousands of Visitors," *Miami Herald*, June 15, 1924.
62. *Miami Daily News*, "County Given an Extension in Beach Case," April 19, 1924.
63. *Miami Herald*, "As It Was—A Famous Ocean Drive Beauty Spot—As It Now Is." *Miami Herald*, June 15, 1924.
64. *Miami Daily News-Metropolis*, "Women Would Tear Down Barriers on Ocean Road," July 9, 1924.
65. Memo, W.A. Kohlhepp to Carl Fisher, July 28, 1924, Fisher Papers, HistoryMiami.
66. *Miami Daily News-Metropolis*, "Judge Denies Stay Against Beach Growth," July 1, 1924.
67. *Miami Herald*, "The News at Miami Beach," July 2, 1924.

68. Flannery, "Miami's Scenic Highway."
69. Vernon Lamme, *Florida Lore Not Found in the History Books* (Boynton Beach FL: Star Publishing, 1973), 82–85.
70. Gordon R. Willey, "Sites in Broward and Dade Counties," *Yale Publications in Anthropology: Florida and Caribbean* (New Haven, CT: Yale University Press, 1949), 79–84.

CHAPTER 6

71. Inflation Calculator, www.dol.gov.
72. F.P. Stockbridge and J.H. Perry, *Florida in the Making* (Kingsport, TN: de Bower Publishing Co., 1926), 153.
73. Hollingsworth, *History of Dade County*, 97.
74. Palm Beach County History, www.pbchistoryonline.org.
75. Correspondence from Carl F. Schoeppl, June 10, 1995, private collection.
76. Hollingsworth, *History of Dade County*, 179–80.
77. *Miami Beach Sun*, "Portraits and Projects of Architects," May 7,1950.
78. *Miami Herald*, Obituary, March 16, 1962.
79. "People of Palm Beach County," www.pbchistoryonline.org.
80. *Miami Herald*, August 8, 1928.
81. Redford, *Billion Dollar Sandbar*, 183.
82. *Miami Herald*, March 12, 14 and 15, 1929, front pages.
83. *Miami Herald*, "Chicagoan Acquires Ocean Front Home," December 27, 1929.
84. Ibid.
85. *Miami Herald*, "Miami Beach Home Planned by Erskine," March 8, 1929.
86. Ibid.
87. *Miami Herald*, "Egbert Gold Leaves $1,509,728 Estate," March 9, 1929.
88. *Miami Herald*, "Fort Wayne Visitor to Build Fine Home," March 11, 1929.
89. *Miami Herald*, "Miami Beach Growth Continues Unabated," August 19, 1928.
90. *Miami Herald*, "Newspaper Owner to Build Home Here," March 5, 1929.
91. Redford, *Billion Dollar Sandbar*, 76.
92. Ibid., 174.
93. *5690 Collins Avenue* (Miami Beach, FL: Brokers Service Bureau, n.d.), HistoryMiami archive.
94. John M. Baker, *American House Styles: A Concise Guide* (New York: W.W. Norton and Co., 1994), 132.
95. *Miami News*, "Laurence Schwab Dies," May 29, 1951.
96. *Society Pictorial*, January 10, 1932, 6.
97. "Briggs Manufacturing Company," www.coachbuilt.com.

98. *Miami Daily News*, "Syndicate Buys Firestone Area," July 21, 1952.
99. U.S. census for Chicago, Illinois, 1930.

CHAPTER 7

100. Stanley Whitman, conversation with the author, February 20, 2014.
101. *Miami Herald*, "Printing Executive Dies After Illness," November 26, 1936.
102. *Sunday Pictorial*, "Marine Room Mirrors Treasures of the Deep," January 10, 1932, 3.
103. www.thegreatautorace.com; www.americanautohistory.com.
104. L.F. Reardon, *The Florida Hurricane & Disaster, 1926* (Coral Gables, FL: Arva Parks & Company; reprint, 1986), 37–38.
105. *Sunday Pictorial*, "Marine Room."
106. Building Permit Card for 4009 Collins Avenue, Miami Beach Building Department.
107. "The Residence of J.C. Penney, Miami, Florida," in *Florida: The East Coast*, 203.
108. *Miami Metropolis*, January 1, 1916.
109. "Residence of J.C. Penney," 203–05.
110. Ibid.
111. *New York Times*, "Dr. J.H. Adams, 74, Author, Inventor," February 10, 1941.
112. *Miami News*, "Adams Rites Set for Today," February 9, 1941.
113. *Florida: The East Coast*, 180.
114. *Miami Herald*, June 11, 1924, 5.
115. *Miami Herald*, "J.H. Adams Leaves for Northern Home," May 14, 1927.
116. "Isle-O-Mar: The Belle Isle Estate of Joseph H. Adams," City of Miami Beach Historical Archive #237, n.d.
117. Joseph H. Adams, *Arthritis and Other Ailments Conquered?* Brochure, 1939.
118. U.S. Census for Dade County, Florida, 1940.
119. "Establishment and Growth of All Souls Described," *Palm Branch* (Diocesan Newsletter, February 1944).
120. *1926 Through 1952: Into Our Second Quarter-Century of Service* (Miami Beach, FL: Committee of One Hundred of Miami Beach, 1952), brochure.
121. *Miami Daily News*, "Star Island's Growth Steady," July 26, 1925.
122. Miami Design Preservation League, "Historic Site Designation Report for 42 Star Island," revised July 16, 2013.
123. "Palm and Hibiscus Islands," in *Florida: The East Coast*, 236.
124. *Florida: The East Coast*, 146.
125. www.Anheuser-Busch.com/history.
126. U.S. census, 1870.
127. *Miami Herald*, Obituary, March 26, 1943, 6-B.

128. Ibid.
129. *Florida: The East Coast*, 93.
130. Ballinger, *Miami Millions*, 47.
131. Ibid.
132. *Miami Daily News & Metropolis*, July 19, 1924.
133. City of Miami Beach Planning Department, "La Gorce Golf Club Historical Evaluation Report," December 11, 2001; revised April 9, 2002.

CHAPTER 8

134. Kleinberg, *Miami Beach*, 51–52.
135. *Miami Herald*, "Miami Beach Growth Continues Unabated," August 19, 1928.
136. *Miami Metropolis*, "Work to Start in Two Weeks on C. Fisher Mansion," August 28, 1914; *Miami Herald*, "Broke Ground on Carl G. Fisher's Residence," October 20, 1914.
137. *Miami Herald*, "May We Present George L. Pfeiffer," July 15, 1936.
138. Prospectus, circa 1925, copy of Fisher correspondence in Kleinberg Papers, City of Miami Beach Historical Archive.
139. Jane Fisher, *Fabulous Hoosier* (New York: McBride & Co., 1947), 127.
140. *Miami Herald*, "New Office Building Opens," November 8, 1923.
141. *Miami Herald*, "E.F. Shepard Dies at Home in Miami Beach," April 11, 1927, front page.
142. www.philadelphiabuildings.org.
143. *Miami Herald*, "Roneys Sue Miami Beach," October 1940, Miami-Dade County Public Library news clipping file.
144. Baker, *American House Styles*, 98.
145. *Florida: The East Coast*, 137.
146. *Miami Metropolis*, "Architectural Ideals in Miami," November 2, 1912; Rodriguez et al., *Wilderness to Metropolis*, 194.
147. *Miami Daily Metropolis*, "Montmare School is to be Started Jan. 10," October 27, 1921.
148. "A Brief History of the Highlights of the Committee of One Hundred. As Told by C.W. Chase Jr. at the Annual Southern Dinner, March 16, 1948," City of Miami Beach Historical Archive, #1074.
149. *1926 through 1952*, brochure.
150. *Miami Metropolis*, "Corporation Formed to Build a Theatre in Miami Beach City," December 19, 1922.
151. *Miami Metropolis*, "Miami Beach People Interested in Theatre," April 10, 1923.

152. *Miami Herald*, May 30, 1925.
153. Hollingsworth, *History of Dade County*, 102.

CHAPTER 9

154. Letter, Carl Fisher to Henry Dutton, August 18, 1921, Fisher correspondence, HistoryMiami.
155. *Miami Herald*, "Apartment House at the Beach Completed," January 21, 1917.
156. Letter, Fisher to Dutton.
157. *Lincoln Hotel*, brochure, Wolfsonian/FIU archive, Miami Beach.
158. *Miami Daily News*, May 12, 1940.
159. Nash, *Magic of Miami Beach*, 121.
160. Redford, *Billion Dollar Sandbar*, 124–25.
161. *Miami Herald*, "Fabled Flamingo Still Flying High," February 29, 1960.
162. *Miami Daily News*, "New York Firm Enters Miami Building Field," July 26, 1925.
163. Rodriguez et al., *Wilderness to Metropolis*, 72.
164. *Miami Herald*, "Nautilus Hotel Honor Roll," January 24, 1924.
165. Kleinberg, *Miami Beach*, 88.
166. *Miami Metropolis*, "Miami Beach Dairy Is Being Moved to Miami," March 24, 1923.
167. *Miami Herald*, "Carl Fisher to Establish Industrial Center at Beach for Colored People," June 12, 1919.
168. *Miami Herald*, "Preparations to Begin Soon for New Auditorium," April 15, 1924.
169. *Miami Herald*, "Miami Beach Garden to Open Tomorrow," January 14, 1925.
170. *Miami News*, "Stage Shows to Be Offered at Auditorium," September 9, 1926.
171. *Miami News*, "Beach Garden Theater Opens," January 16, 1927.
172. *Miami Herald*, March 1–4, 1934.
173. *Miami Daily News*, "King Cole Has Several New Features," July 26, 1925.
174. *The Boulevard*, brochure, Wolfsonian/FIU archive, Miami Beach.

CHAPTER 10

175. *Florida: The East Coast*, 211.
176. *The Book of Florida* (N.p.: James O. Jones, publisher, 1925), 491.
177. Stofik, *Saving South Beach*, 157–58.
178. Kleinberg. *Miami Beach*, 104.

179. *Miami Herald*, "Deauville Casino to Reopen Shortly," January 31, 1928.
180. *Miami News*, "M'Fadden-Deauville Blaze Darkens Beach," December 23, 1956.
181. *Florida: The East Coast*, 161.
182. Ibid., 20.
183. Ibid., 210.
184. Advertisement, *Miami Herald*, December 16, 1923.
185. *Miami Herald*, Obituary, June 16, 1950.
186. City of Miami Beach Historical Archive, #1680-24.
187. *Miami News*, July 8, 1924.
188. Ibid., August 14, 1922.
189. *Miami Daily News and Metropolis*, "Famed Seaside Rendezvous Ready," February 7, 1926.
190. Donald Curl, *Mizner's Florida* (New York: Architectural History Foundation, 1984).
191. Helen Wells, "Dick Mead Banks on Miami," *Miami Herald*, February 12, 1963.
192. *Miami Herald*, "Lansburgh Buys a Hotel to Level It," March 7, 1963.
193. *Miami Herald* and *Miami Daily News*, Roy France Obituaries, February 17, 1972.
194. Ibid.
195. Kleinberg, *Miami Beach*, 210.
196. Ibid., 211.

SELECTED BIBLIOGRAPHY

Ballinger, Kenneth. *Miami Millions: The Dance of the Dollars in the Great Florida Land Boom of 1925*. Miami, FL: Franklin Press Inc., 1936.

Building Records. City of Miami Beach Building Department.

Carson, Ruby Leach. "Forty Years of Miami Beach." *Tequesta* 15 (1955).

Florida: The East Coast. Miami, FL: Miami Herald Publishing Co., ca. 1924.

Hollingsworth, Tracy. *History of Dade County Florida.* Coral Gables, FL: Parker Art Printing, 1949.

Kleinberg, Howard. *Miami Beach: A History*. Miami, FL: Centennial Press, 1994.

———. *Woggles and Cheese Holes: The History of Miami Beach's Hotels*. Miami Beach, FL: Greater Miami and the Beaches Hotel Association, 2005.

Lavender, Abraham D. *Miami Beach in 1920: The Making of a Winter Resort.* Charleston SC: Arcadia Publishing, 2002.

Nash, Charles E. *The Magic of Miami Beach*. Philadelphia: David McKay Co., 1938.

SELECTED BIBLIOGRAPHY

Pierce, Charles W. *Pioneer Life in Southeast Florida*. Coral Gables, FL: University of Miami Press, 1970.

Redford, Polly. *Billion Dollar Sandbar: A Biography of Miami Beach*. New York: E.P. Dutton & Co., 1970.

Rodriguez, I., M. Ammidown and E.P. Dieterich. *From Wilderness to Metropolis*. Miami, FL: Metropolitan Dade County Division of Historic Preservation, 1992.

Stearns, Frank. *Along Greater Miami's Sun-Sea-Ara*. Miami, FL: F.F. Stearns, 1932.

Stofik, M. Barron. *Saving South Beach*. Gainesville: University Press of Florida, 2005.

Index

K

L

M

N

O

P

R

About the Author

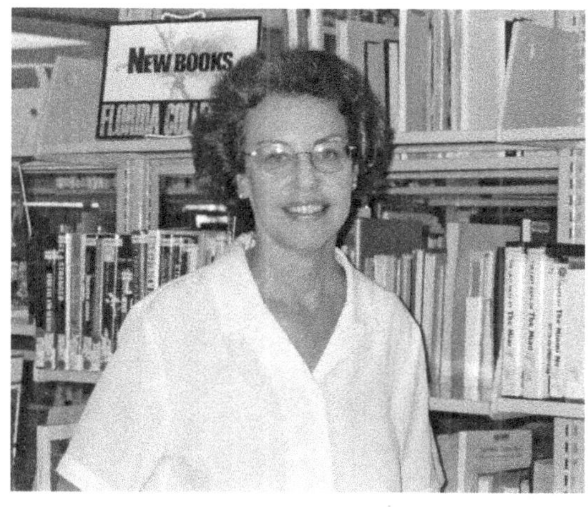

Carolyn Klepser, a graduate of Beloit (Wisconsin) College and New York Medical College, had a first career as a nurse in New York City and overseas with the Peace Corps. After many Florida vacations and too many northern winters, she moved to Miami Beach in 1994. A lifelong interest in history and architecture led her to nearly twenty years of researching the city's older buildings, both for local architects and as a consultant to the City of Miami Beach, assisting in the designation of many of the city's historic districts and sites. With Miami historian Arva Moore Parks, she co-authored *Miami Then and Now* in 2002 and a revised edition in 2014 (Anova Books). She currently lives by Lake Pancoast in Miami Beach and works part time in cardiology.

www.ingramcontent.com/pod-product-compliance
Lightning Source LLC
LaVergne TN
LVHW052341100826
845147LV00021B/1139
* 9 7 8 1 6 2 6 1 9 4 2 8 1 *